How to Prosper
in the Coming Good Years

How to Prosper in the Coming GOOD Years

Larry R. Williams

REGNERY GATEWAY

Published by Regnery Gateway
360 West Superior Street
Chicago, Illinois 60610

Library of Congress Catalog Card Number: 81-52141
International Standard Book Number: 0-89526-667-9

Manufactured in the United States of America

To Kelly, Sara, Jason, Shelly, and Carla
who have made my years so prosperous

Contents

Introduction

Nothing sells like success. In the past, this old adage used to mean that nothing sells like bullish, positive investment advice. In fact, when I first entered the investment advisory publishing business, I was told by virtually all the old-timers to leave off forecasting doom and gloom; they said there simply wasn't any money in it and such forecasting would not increase my list of subscribers substantially.

But all this seemed to change around 1966, when suddenly a group of investment advisers became very successful with just such a line: the world, and our monetary system, were on the brink of chaos, they said, and disaster was just around the corner.

I do not believe this, and so I have written this book with two explicit purposes in mind: first, to prove conclusively that America is *not* falling apart at the seams; and second, to demonstrate what I believe the best investment opportunities will be over the next ten to twenty years. Things are going to get *better*, not worse, and with this in mind the astute and optimistic investor will have a very good chance of reaping substantial rewards. He may even become very, very rich.

Evolutionary Economics

Almost without exception, economists attempt to predict the future economic situation based on past data—on what the economy *has* done in the past. Because of this they have tended to ignore a most important law of the market. That law I call Evolutionary Economics. Without an understanding of Evolutionary Economics, it's all too easy to fall into the doom-and-gloom view; for what the law of Evolutionary Economics shows is that the economic condition of the world progresses, moving from good to better.

Economic evolution is very similar to human evolution. In the past, man led a pretty good life, even though he only lived

1

to be twenty-five or so and rarely grew to a height of more than five feet. There was nothing wrong with this; it suited man in past times. But men and women have evolved from that point to a life expectancy that now is edging closer to eighty, and have grown to an average height now of close to six feet. Economic evolution has resulted in much the same situation: things have gotten progressively better as man himself has progressed.

Contrast, if you will, life a century ago with life today. A century ago there was no indoor plumbing, no central heating or air-conditioning, inadequate refrigeration for food; looking back it all seems rather unpleasant. However, life one century ago was substantially better than life *two* centuries ago.

We can see the same thing in the American marketplace over the last thirty years. Now, it has become very popular and fashionable to belittle the quality of present-day workmanship in this country; perhaps the brunt of this criticism has been directed at the automobile. But again, without a doubt the 1980 American automobile is a more convenient, workable, and efficient vehicle than the 1950 automobile. And just as the 1980 car is better than the 1950 car, so the 1950 car was more craftsman-like and certainly more comfortable than the original Model T.

If economic, political, and social history teaches us nothing else, it should teach us that, in fact, things get better on this planet and not worse. The world revolves in the same way it did one hundred years ago; standards of living rise; and based on this alone I must conclude that the best approach in the next twenty years regarding economic matters is an optimistic and adventurous one.

I am not saying that there will not be bad times within the good times; there will be, of course, there always are. So I would like to limit my broad optimistic approach to certain specific matters which indicate that the 1980's will be a time of great economic opportunity.

Taking a Chance

It would be sophomoric to assume that we can predict good times ahead merely from the results of the 1980 presidential election; while the majority of prognosticators believe Reagan's economic policy will prove sound, we cannot rely on such guesswork alone. There are other reasons for economic optimism, though I grant you would not know this from the popular economics manuals which have occupied the best-sellers' list these last few years. Mr. Howard Ruff, the most successful of the current nay-sayers, is forecasting a recession in the very near future, which will be "as deep," he says, "or deeper, than 1974." "Real estate prices," Ruff continues, "and interest rates will crash, long-term bonds will have one of the most spectacular market rallies in history, while government panic spending will keep away any full-scale depression, but *barely*, by the skin of their teeth." And, if by now you are not sufficiently frightened, Ruff delivers a crushing blow: "Then inflation will take off to unheard-of levels of 40% a year and more."

Ruff leads, and many others follow. After he correctly predicted the course of gold and silver prices in the late 1970's and early '80s, and after his successful declaration that inflation would go into a spiral, the American public demanded, and got, a new breed of investment advisors committed to an apocalyptic view of the future of this country. No matter that other, more optimistic investment advisors made similar forecasts; Ruff got the publicity, and the law of supply-and-demand was in full force. As a result, many investors are now operating with the belief that we are trapped in an ever-expanding inflationary spiral which can only lead to a second Great Depression; and I find this sort of thinking unfortunate and not to the point.

Glen King Parker, who publishes the newsletter *Market Logic*, has presented the most telling evidence that matters are not at all as serious as we have been led to believe. In his December, 1980, issue, Parker contrasted the inflationary rate of Weimar Germany with the inflationary rate today. In the 1920's, Germany's inflation was skyrocketing at a rate of 3,500% per month. 3,500%! America is, I am happy to report, in slightly better circumstances; we have an inflation rate of 9% a year.

Are our problems truly insoluble? Of course not. As Parker discovered, the Weimar inflation was brought to a halt, and not within years, or even months, but rather in a matter of days. How? Simple: the government stopped printing new money. Once the *D-Mark* was again backed by gold and agricultural parity, the debacle was over and Germany found itself on solid footing once again. I realize that some astute professor of economics may object and say that backing the dollar with gold and ridding our government of a Keynesian perspective are hopelessly old fashioned remedies for a very modern problem. That may be; but why is it old remedies are thought to have no potency? Japan used this same old-fashioned remedy to correct its economy in the last decade, and it worked very well.

In 1974, inflation rates in Japan stood at approximately 25%—again, a rate much more serious and dangerous than our own. But by 1978 inflation stood at 3% in Japan merely because the monetary authorities began printing less currency. They instituted monetary restraint, and immediately inflation fell. And it should be noted that inflation declined just at the time when OPEC had raised the price of oil to such exorbitant levels. Clearly, the cost of energy has little relation to inflation; *inflation is directly dependent on the weakness of a country's currency.*

The key point here is that *inflation will occur only when the money supply is increased at a rate faster than the rate of productivity.* When this happens, you have inflation; when it does not happen, you do not have inflation. The sooner our Federal Reserve System backs the dollar with gold, or begins adjusting our money supply figures based not on their whims and political orthodoxy but on production index figures, the sooner we will rid ourselves of our inflationary spiral. Still, *even if* inflation reaches 20%, as Howard Ruff predicts, it can be lowered, and instantaneously, as was the case in Weimar Germany and in Japan. In England, Mrs. Thatcher cut back the money supply in her first months in office and inflation indices were cut in half. Unfortunately, the success of this policy led Mrs. Thatcher to become rather sanguine, to ease restraints, and the inflation figures began to spiral again. We cannot let such a thing happen in America; once a proper policy is enacted, we must see it through.

We all want to improve our lot and our surroundings; this is the simple truth upon which Evolutionary Economics is based, and it is the truth which the doom-sayers have either ignored or forgotten. Will we come again to recognize this truth in the 1980's? Has our time come?

How the Stock Market Fits In

It is now a universally recognized fact that there is a powerful decennial pattern to our economy: In the first two years of a decade, stock market prices fall, and in the third rise again strongly (as measured by the Dow Jones Industrial Average) and remain high through the end of the decade.

My years as an investment advisor have taught me that the Dow Jones Average is a superb indicator of the future economic activity of this country. In fact, stock prices usually predate economic turnabouts in America by three to six months, and in some cases up to a year. A rise in the Dow Jones average is a sign of advancement in our economic climate, and a dip in the Dow Jones is a sign of economic retreat. This becomes very clear when you look at the following chart, in which the Dow Jones is superimposed on the rate of change in our Industrial Production Index.

This is not incidental. Truly astute investors do their homework, to know approximately when economic conditions are going to improve. They know also that as economic conditions improve, stock prices will rise. Therefore, they purchase stock *in advance* of an economic turnaround; they buy stock cheaply, then sell it when the price rises and stock is in demand.

They are thus taking advantage of the short-sightedness of most people. When the canny investors buy stock in expectation that it will rise in value and careful consideration of the market potential, they inspire not trust but cynicism. There rises what is known in the market as "contrary opinion," by means of which market prices remain low for a while: "If everyone thinks this stock is going to rise, you can bet that it will not rise; I will lose my shirt if I go in for it." So, when the majority of investors are bullish—excessively optimistic— about stock prices and insist they will rise, the immediate reaction in the market is a decrease in general stock value. And

Chart 1
Stock Prices Superimposed upon the Rate of Industrial Production Growth

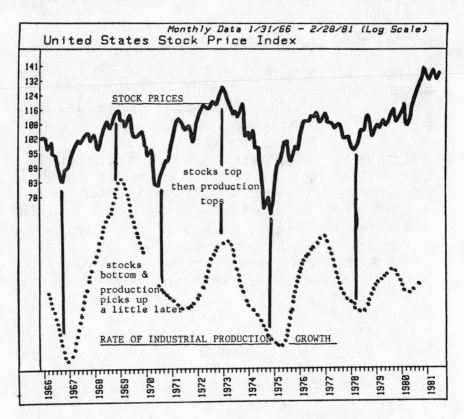

Monthly Data 1/31/66 - 2/28/81 (Log Scale)

United States Stock Price Index

STOCK PRICES

stocks top
then production
tops

stocks
bottom &
production
picks up
a little later

RATE OF INDUSTRIAL PRODUCTION   GROWTH

when the majority of investors are excessively bearish—full of gloom—and are convinced prices will decline, prices rise. Thus, economic data allows us to measure the fluctuations in mood that result from investor optimism or pessimism.

Now, if a poll were taken at this very moment, I doubt that the majority of regular investors would be feeling either optimistic or pessimistic; financial matters are too unsure at the moment, and everyone is watching carefully as Reagan attempts to introduce his budgetary and tax policies. But the market-place has *itself* taken a poll, and clearly the theoreticians of the apocalypse have won. The sudden and unprecedented popularity of such investment advisors as James Dines, Howard Ruff, Harry Schultz, and Verne Meyer is testimony to the firm hold they have on the imagination of the public; public *sentiment* is pessimistic in general, and that sentiment has made these forecasters very wealthy in the last five years. However, the game would be over if these forecasts were right, for the stock market and the economy would never again change for the better. We know that fluctuation is at the very heart of all stock-market activity. On this basis alone, I think we can safely conclude that the gloomy, pessimistic trend has had its day, and that these particular investors will be caught off guard and left in the dust when the demise and destruction they have been counting on never takes place.

They tell us that America is out of control, that America will not be able to regain control, and, therefore, that economic and monetary systems the world over are going to collapse. There is a small measure of truth to this view: America is not in economic control (in fact, most often it never is in economic control). Government interference and the desire of many to play the safest hand possible have prevented the free market from taking command in these days. But, if we are out of control, there is no reason we cannot regain control. It was not due to the conjuction of certain stars or the exercising of power by a mysterious force that led us to our somewhat unhappy present situation—blame is much more easily apportioned, to politicians and economists. And certainly whatever man does he can subsequently undo.

A belief in economic predestination is gripping this country:

President Reagan was elected and supply-side economics can be put into effect, yet somehow, there is a distinct feeling among people that the situation is hopeless and that we are soon to find ourselves in a major Depression. Let me make it clear; I do not think we are immune from Depression. In fact, it is my personal opinion that we *will* see a major economic disaster afflict this country in the not-too-distant future (this is discussed later in this book). But we should not be paralyzed by this; it may *not* happen, and besides, I believe we have at least twenty good years ahead in which to invest wisely and optimistically, and in which to make a good deal of money. If we wait around for the crisis, always wary of it looking over our shoulder, we will not make good investments and fortunes will pass through our fingers.

In fact, fortunes have already been trickling away, due to the success of the pessimistic Ruffians. Ruff and his crowd have advised their customers to invest in cash, diamonds, and gold. Now, cash value has been eroding, due to inflation; gold has fluctuated wildly in the past five years, and could again sink extraordinarily low at any time. We know from the case of the Hunt brothers that investment in metals is no guarantee of safe passage through troubled waters. Even diamonds have not fared well in 1980–81. Make no mistake, though, Howard Ruff is a brilliant man, who understands the Free Market system . . . who has fought for it . . . and, in his own way, has made a positive change in this country's direction. He is one of the people responsible for the return to "Good Times". At this point, he may not see it, yet, but the good days are coming; and, in part, due to Ruff's dedication and principles, which he has helped reestablish in economic societies.

Consider, instead, the person who bought shares of stock in any of the oil companies, in almost any of the medical research companies, or even invested his capital in good real-estate opportunities. In the last five years there have been some stupendous economic returns in these fields that defy any previous standards of exponential growth. We do have the advantage of hindsight, I admit, and can see that these have proved sound investments only after the fact; but this is the only perspective from which we can evaluate such matters.

And while the pessimistic investor did make some money on his gold, he earned nowhere near as much as the optimistic investor with his oil and medical stocks.

It is said that the virtue of pessimism is that when you are proved wrong you are very pleasantly surprised. However, to be pessimistic in these days is to be left on the sidelines, no richer and not reaping the joys of a pleasant surprise. If you are an optimist, and wrong, you will be broke anyway. If you are a pessimist, and right, you will be broke; as if you are a pessimist, and you are proved wrong, again you will be broke.

"New Issues"

The beauty of the world of economics and investments is that one can always look back to see what, in fact, has been working the best. Call it "Monday morning quarter-backing" if you like; but it really isn't, in that we *can* actually see what would have been the best strategy. We now have the hindsight to look back and see what would have been better, buying stocks or buying gold; buying real estate or buying JOJOBA Bean Futures. Unlike so many of mankind's activities, we are fortunate in that the investment world is chock-full of facts, figures and numbers; and we have those numbers to evaluate performance.

If we were to do that, and evaluate the performance of stocks versus gold, as just one example, I think you might be surprised to see how well stocks have fared.

Glen King Parker also publishes *New Issues*, a market letter that focuses on newly listed stocks. He began publishing the letter in 1979, and during that time period, has recommended 85 new issues for purchase. The average gain of those 85 issues has been 115%, which is a tremendous return on your money. There were only two stocks that performed poorly: Sanders Technology, which lost 42% in value, and Brae, which lost 46% in value. On the up-side, however, Avantek had a gain of 1,206%; Brock Hotel had a 203% gain; Brookwood Health had a 16% gain; Compact Video had a 410% gain; Evans and Sutherland had an 891% gain; ISC Systems had a 310% gain; Microdyne had a 270% gain; NBI had a 360% gain; Sci-Tex had a 277% gain; Spectradyne had a 318% gain; and Unit Drilling had a 264% gain; as well as Federal Express, which showed a 1,000% gain.

Clearly, there has been opportunity in not only listed stocks, which represent the vested interest in America; but, more importantly, in the growth stocks, the stocks that are just going public, such as the *New Issues* market letter discusses. There have not only been incredible gains in the price of the stocks, but some amazing fortunes made; fortunes that will last several generations. I expect the majority of these stocks will continue performing as spectacularly in the future as they have in the past.

Now, I ask you, which is better? To take a chance, with the possibility that you are wrong, or to be safe, and stay away from the action? The optimist is the winner in either case.

Bear or Bull?

The great problem of being a perpetual Bear is that you will never be happy, never really satisfied until the economy does "crackup," until the Great Depression comes, and gold hits your mystical number, whether it's $1,000 an ounce or $40,000 an ounce. Until then, all along the way, you will not be happy. You will not have attained your goal. Compare that, if you will, with the person who has an optimistic, or Bullish, view. He is happy consistently along the way. Sure, he realizes that, from time to time, there will be economic setbacks, that there are no straight roads to Heaven. Nevertheless, he can take these as they come; whereas the Bearish person, who will continually have Bull markets against him, will see these as problems, totally unacceptable to the ultimate goal of destruction.

The optimist, of course, can survive without destruction, and continue to find psychological fulfillment in that there is no ultimate goal. His goal is to make money in the markets and in the economy. He need not be concerned with the final "crackup," the final day of reckoning or judgement. That never crosses his mind. If it occurs, we are all going to be in the same boat, whether optimist or pessimist; but along the way, the optimist will be psychologically fulfilled. He will see his goals attained along the way. He will see Bull markets and, even if they are only Bull markets within an overall down trend, he will at least be fulfilled at those points.

But, the Bear will only be fulfilled on a psychologically emotional basis only once, and that can only come on a total economic destruction of the economy. The chances of that occurring are very slim, when you consider it's only happened once in the history of this country; and that may, in fact, be only once in the history of recent modern man. The Bullish person, however, is continually fulfilled along the way, as he sees the economy take its up-turns and business profits, from time to time.

So why not join the good times?

1

The Good News

First, the Old Bad News

At the risk of over-simplification, I think it's safe to say the bad news, in terms of present-day economics, was having Jimmy Carter as President. The good news will come, not necessarily from having Ronald Reagan as President but from having *anyone* other than Jimmy Carter.

The best good news is going to come from three main areas: inflation, unemployment, and the ability of the average American to improve the quality of his life-style. If you've been doing your homework, you have perhaps noticed that there have been several economic forecasts, from some of the best forecasters in the business, which make the same important point: the '80s will be a substantially better time than the '70s.

Perhaps it's a question of philosophy, but when you consider that Paul Volcker, the current head of the Federal Reserve System, said a few years ago that "the American living standard has got to decline," you can only wonder at the mentality of the Carter administration regarding any kind of economic development whatsoever in the 1980s.

You do have to give Paul Volcker credit for one thing: he acted on his belief and his prediction. Interest rates rose from 11% to 22% under his guidance, and inflation rose from 11% to almost 20%. Worse yet, there was a 10% decline in worker consumption and a 50% decline in the auto and construction industries. All in all, there was a more than 8% decline in production. That was the bad news at the tail end of the '70s.

Our Friend, the Prime Rate

The first bad news comes from the Prime Lending Rate: the quickest way to put the brakes on American business is to raise the Prime, which is, of course, exactly what happened. And once you put the brakes on American business the next prob-

13

lem that comes up to plague the U.S. economy is unemployment. It's pretty clear that the higher the interest rate, the higher the unemployment we have in this country. What makes high unemployment particularly excruciating is what we see happening because of it to the Consumer Price Index. When things cost a great deal, due to high interest rates and high unemployment, things in general cost more, and that is painful. Domestic auto production declines, housing construction and sales decline, and steel production declines. That's what we would see in a chart graphing the consumption of the Productive Work Force. Consumption will go down from some $204 billion in 1980 to a projected $165 billion in 1982 unless some major changes are made in the nation's economy. The decade past ended on a sour note indeed. During the '70s real Gross National Product grew at a 2½% rate annually; during the '60s, by contrast, real GNP growth rates stood at 6%.

Moving Ahead by Looking Backward

It is important that the investor, and the person concerned with the economic stability and growth of this country, know what we've been through. If they do know this, they will come to realize that the next, most logical move should be in the opposite direction and that, in fact, many of the economic problems we've had have not been the results of cyclical economic phenomena but rather of presidential and political phenomena. That may well be best demonstrated by the course taken by the Dow Jones Industrial Average during the Carter years. When Carter took office, the Dow Jones stood at 974.92. Yet some four years later, the Dow Jones came to rest around 940. It would appear that investors did not give the President that hard a time, nor did Carter give them too much trouble. But if you take into account the gargantuan inflation of those four years, you see that the Dow Jones should have risen to 1412.9 for investors to keep even with the 1976 figure! This is proof positive of just how disastrous the Carter economic policies really were. Given the above dismal figures, the pessimistic, concerned investor is bound to wonder whether it will be possible for things to change in the 1980s. Have we gone past the point of no return, or, if some change is possible, will it be a long time in coming? A pessimist would, of course, answer the last question in the affirmative; nothing can be done, the problem has just gotten too big. Nothing by one man, nothing by one part, and certainly nothing by one vote.

Voting Works: Look at Puerto Rico

While that may be a popular view, those of us who are concerned with the future have studied the past; and based on that, the obvious conclusion is that things do, indeed, change. People can make a difference, and we will see changes in the '80s. One radical change occurred just recently inside this country: the Proposition 13 movement led by my friend Howard Jarvis in California. Within the twelve months following the passage of Proposition 13, there were an additional half-million new jobs in California and the rate of inflation had risen less than in any other major state. In short, a substantial economic change—a massive tax cut—produced a predictable positive response in the state's economy. As more and more people came to have more and more money in their pockets, the economy was stimulated, which meant more and more jobs. More production meant more goods, to be bought by the people with more money. Hence, this amounted to a substantial reversal of the inflationary spiral.

But one may argue that *one* tax cut in *one* state alone is not conclusive proof that things can everywhere be changed for the better.

If that's the way you feel, I suggest you turn your attention to Puerto Rico. In 1976, Carlos Romero–Barcelo won an important gubernatorial victory by pledging to slash taxes and institute massive economic stimuli to business. His first priority was to take apart the bureaucracy bit by bit, reduce taxes and thus stimulate the economy. You may well say that he has already done what Ronald Reagan has promised to do in the first part of the '80s. We've seen a small Ronald Reagan scenario already at work in the Western hemisphere and the results have been spectacular.

As you first read the words "Puerto Rico" you probably had

the typical stereotype in your mind: a place in dire economic straits from which the natives were fleeing to New York City to escape mass poverty. Now that's been reversed, and Puerto Ricans are migrating *from* New York City *back to* Puerto Rico because economic conditions there are better than in the Big Apple. Puerto Rican income taxes have been reduced 5% a year since 1977, with predictable results: increased productivity, more jobs and a better life-style for all. The creator of the Romero–Barcelo tax reduction is the brilliant Arthur Laffer, one of Reagan's key economists.

Why a Tax Cut Stimulates the Economy

In 1963, the highest marginal tax rate was 91%, with the lowest at 20%. President Kennedy took a bold step forward and reduced the highest rate by 70% and the lowest by 14%. In other words, he reduced taxation most radically for those in the highest tax bracket—the really big wage earners—and not so much for people at the lower end. Kennedy even went one step further: he cut the Corporate Tax Rate from 52% to 46%. The unemployment rate fell from 6¾% to 4%. The Federal Budget roughly balanced itself. This is the model upon which the Kemp–Roth 30%–three year plan is based. It has one other immeasurable advantage: inflation averaged between 1% and 2% after the Kennedy cut. Ronald Reagan wants to try the same proposal now; if he succeeds, similar results should follow.

Note that in all the examples I've given here, the tax cuts had an immediate positive impact: in the case of Proposition 13, less than 12 months; in Puerto Rico, less than 18 months; in the Kennedy period, less than 14 months. Reagan's policies should be as rapidly effective, and will produce an immediate and substantial change within the investment community.

DRI, or Happy Days are Here Again

Perhaps the most comprehensive forecast of what the Reagan victory holds in store for business was carried out by Data Resources Incorporated (DRI), of Lexington, Massachusetts.

The firm uses a 900-factor model of the economy to forecast trends in interest rates, consumer spending, unemployment, credit expansion and contraction. Their methods are painstaking and irreproachable: when dealing with the housing industry, for example, they look not only at housing starts but include mobile home shipments, stocks of homes and mobile homes, and the inventory of unsold single-family homes as well. They measure personal consumption in forty-one different ways, while looking at automobile sales from thirty-five different perspectives.

DRI took their exhaustive computer model and plugged in the Kemp–Roth tax cut, to gauge its potential effect on the economy. The result: if the cut goes into effect, we will have a quick economic recovery. The econometric model suggests the average growth rate of the GNP will rise to almost 4%, picking up from the 2½% pace we've been seeing. The average citizen will have more money in his pockets because of the tax reductions, and as a result the DRI survey forecasts a substantially higher per capita disposable income. In other words, the average American is going to have more money to do with as he pleases if the tax cut is implemented.

What to Do with All Our Money

As far as investing goes, most investors are most familiar with the stock market, and know that what makes stock market prices rise most quickly and for the longest period are profits. In fact, my fifteen years' experience in forecasting the stock market shows that the number-one force behind rising stock prices is a belief among investors that the profits of a given corporation are going to increase.

The DRI forecast shows that after-tax profits for corporations, given the implementation of the Reagan program, would skyrocket to almost $100 billion by 1984. (For comparison's sake, their forecast of Jimmy Carter's economic program would have shown an increase of only some $78 billion.) So, the GNP will not only rise more quickly, but corporate after-tax profits will grow in value as well because of the increase in the GNP. Specifically, the DRI forecast shows that after-tax profits in 1981 should be approximately $70 billion, almost $80 billion by 1982, $87 billion by 1983, and more than $90 billion by 1984.

Money Means More Jobs—
And More Money

All this makes nice reading for the investor, but when it comes to the man in the street, who may not be a J.P. Morgan, there are two other factors rising out of the DRI survey that offer nothing but hope for his future. First, the unemployment rate should, according to the computer, decline from 8.6% in 1981 to 6.9% by 1984, so there should be more jobs as the decade progresses. And second, and best yet, we should also have less inflation.

This may seem perplexing, since in recent years political economics has dictated that if we stimulate the economy and put more money in circulation and in the consumers' pockets, inflation will only go up. Computer print-outs clearly say, however, that that's not the case. Inflation currently runs rampant at almost 20%; the model forecasts an inflation rate of approximately 10%.

It may be you are starting to wonder why you should trust this DRI survey, with its boundlessly optimistic findings. Well, let's toss the survey out for a moment and turn to some serious and distinguished academic economists, who have been painting the real picture of the coming economic boom. Men like Eli Ginzberg of Columbia University, Walter Heller, the former chairman of Kennedy's Council of Economic Advisors, and even the very liberal Otto Eckstein have taken up what is now thought of as the "conservative," "Republican" economic philosophy behind the tax cut. Ginzberg and Heller are even looking forward to real "fat years" ahead.

The Business Boomlet

One of the most significant developments in the economic community today is the consolidation of business and labor. They are uniting—not much, but still they are uniting—so that together they can compete against foreign products in the

American market and overseas. Because of this, our hold on the foreign market should expand; we have at last come to realize that quality is as important as quantity in production. The quality of American products has been improving: the demise of the gas guzzler is the best sign of this. It also shows up in improvements on every product from textiles to bottle lids.

Edward Greenberg, a professor of economics at Washington University in St. Louis, says that business will now be devoting less of its attention to environmental regulations, which have been a stumbling-block to growth. "Many firms," Greenberg writes, "can now devote themselves to seeking technological innovations." Together, all this is to the good as far as business is concerned.

More for Everyone, via the Stock Market

If you stop to think about it, you're bound to see valid reasons yourself why the economy will improve. For a moment, reflect on the fact that the birth rate in this country has been on the decline for the last fifteen years. This fact has great and grave economic implications: there will be more money to spend on the dwindling number of children who *are* born. Politically it is significant because it means we will not have to continue the financially ruinous expansion of school systems throughout the country. Schools will either require less money from the taxpayer or will use the moneys they have at their disposal on things other than brick buildings. All this, simply because there will not be as many students, or as many children, in the '80s and '90s as there were in the '60s and '70s.

Perhaps this is why Louis Rukeyser, the gnome of "Wall Street Week," has declared that "the 1980s will be the decade of common stocks." Rukeyser has gone on record saying that he too sees lower inflation, improving U.S. productivity and greater receptivity to business profits over the coming years. Apparently Rukeyser thinks that capitalism will no longer be the dirty word it was in the 1970s, and, on that basis alone, sees higher stock prices. While the media headlines and the list of recent best-selling financial books have painted a picture of doom and gloom, ranging from depression to chaos, Rukeyser has said: "Against all the contrary evidence the country is going to muddle through and the investments that will benefit most from that startling survival will be equities." That, of course, means the stock market.

We need to direct our attention away from the national scene for just a moment and look at what has been taking place in the individual states throughout the country as well. Already the tax reduction movement has moved east from the shores of California to Idaho, Minnesota and Montana. It is now reaching the Atlantic coast, where Massachusetts has passed substantial tax-cut legislation, and to Delaware, which has lowered its phenomenally high progressive rate from 19.8% to 13.5%. So not only will people have more money in their pockets because of Federal tax cut, but because of state tax cuts as well. That stimulates the economy. It puts more money into the hands of investors, who can take advantage of the "decade of common stock" and make themselves a killing.

The Economic Law of the Totem Pole

The fundamental principle of the Reagan economic philosophy is that when conditions improve for people at the high end or the middle of the economic spectrum, they will also improve for those at the lower end. This is a goal worth fighting for; it is, in fact, a cause. However, it is not the only economic cause; some economists, in the name of a worthy cause, have been attempting to repeal a basic law of economics, and have, of course, been unsuccessful. This I have called "the totem pole law." Quite simply put, there has to be a bottom to everything: regardless of how tall your totem pole is, how beautiful it is, or where it is located, there will always be a top to it, a middle to it, and a bottom. There is nothing to be done about this other than acknowledge its truth. Some political and economic people, however, have been trying to deny it, and have been trying to remove the bottom of the totem pole through legislation and theorizing. The results have been all too predictable; no matter what happens, the totem pole *still* has a bottom. All you do when you try to change its structure is undermine its stability. Fortunately, the new administration is concerned with improving the quality of the entire totem pole, not trying to repeal the laws of gravity or physics.

The Money Supply Goes on a Diet

Additional good news comes from the Bank Credit Analyst in Montreal, Canada, who has pointed out that real world money supply—the amount of money in circulation throughout the world—has been shrinking since 1979. If real world money supply continues to shrink, not radically but gradually, and at the same time production increases throughout the globe, we'll have the best of both worlds. Fewer dollars will be buying more and more goods, which means lower prices, which means lower inflation. This is important evidence of a worldwide economic upswing.

No Matter What Happens, It Has to Get Better—
The UCLA Business Forecasting Project

If you still have doubts, you might enjoy reading a December 15, 1980 *Wall Street Journal* article. Reporters John Andrew and Ed Moosbrugger took a trip to the University of California at Los Angeles (UCLA) Business Forecasting Project. There they used a computer to measure the effect twelve simultaneous economic changes would have on the economy for the next two years. The program called for a 13% increase in military spending (more radical than Reagan's proposal), as well as a 50% increase in oil prices. Both these factors were plugged into the model, and the outcome was not disastrous at all. In fact, the only major impact was a 7% drop in retail car sales.

Reporter John Andrew wanted to see, further, what impact would be felt if the growth rate of federal funds were firm at 18% over the next two years, while at the same time the growth rate of capital expenditures were held at zero. Again, the model forecasted some change—housing would be down, for example—but there would be no Apocalypse. The men who developed the computer model, Robert Williams (no relation to yours truly, the author) and Larry Kimbel, say that the only thing they think would throw the economy into darkness would be an increase by OPEC of oil prices to $500 a barrel.

"The economy," Kimbel says, "is surprisingly resilient." Indeed it is. Mathematically speaking, the numbers for the last few years have been so horrible that incoming data can only be better. This is not to say that things can't worsen in the near-future; there is always that possibility. But the mathematical equations we've been dealing with do not suggest that will take place.

The Double-Barrelled, Optimistic Shotgun

When it comes to making investment decisions and trying to forecast what is coming in the next three years, I'm not nearly as interested in computerized models as I am in the way the economy is going to be run and in those who will be running it. The cabinet President Reagan has chosen, as well as his economic advisors, all seem the type of people to push through the important and workable economic program the administration has been talking about.

The majority of the states will be adopting Reagan's economic policies, that seems clear. Accordingly, then, we will be seeing those states reducing taxes and allowing environmentally sound production policies to continue in the states. Thus we're looking into a double-barrelled optimistic shotgun: not only does the economy get assistance from the federal level, but from the state level as well. We investors should take heart; good times are coming.

2

Gold Doesn't Always Glitter and Diamonds May Not Be a Girl's Best Friend

No Sure Thing

What the usual hard-money boys consider the best investments today—gold, diamonds and silver—are in fact, as risky
and speculative as any other sort of investment. I will do everything I can in the next few pages to show you why, over the
coming years, there may *not* be a surge that will drive the prices
of these metals even higher.

Gold

But just because I am somewhat down on gold, please do not
think that I am anti-gold. I've been as bullish on gold as most
any of the bears have been. It's just that investments go into
and out of fashion, and gold is, I think, on its way out. What is
going to take place economically in this country over the next
four years, courtesy of President Reagan, may well mean the
end of the gold boom.

My first contact with gold as an investment came in the
mid-1960s: the Federal Reserve System put on a demonstration
for investment advisors and stock brokers, to show them what
the future trend of gold would most likely be. As far as Federal
Reserve "show-and-tell" ceremonies go, it was superb. There
were flip charts; there was an overhead projector; there were
graphs; there were scales; there were statistics gathered from
all over the world. The net line of all the charts, graphs and
numbers, was that gold was slightly overpriced at $38 an ounce
and would most likely fall down to the $20 an ounce area. I'll
never forget that afternoon. First I started to buy the line; it was
very impressive to watch leading economic advisors and members of the Federal Reserve System write out all these figures
showing what should take place in the gold market. I was
sitting in the back of the room with an old-time investor, who

turned to me when the performance was over and said, "Any time that the Federal Reserve System of the United States of America has got to put on a dog and pony show like this, you better believe what they're saying is not what is going to happen."

I reflected a great deal on what my friend told me; and the more I thought about it, the more I realized that something was wrong. If, in fact, the Federal Reserve System felt so pressured that they had to put on this production for the people who were advising other people about the future economic conditions, I concluded, along with my friend, that the price of gold would go up, not down.

Three Reasons Why Gold Skyrocketed

And indeed it did. It went up, not down, for many reasons, which can be boiled down to three major problems. The first was the tremendous increase in printing-press dollars that cheapened the value of our dollar. It was well said that the price of gold did not go up, the value of the dollar went down. It still takes about the same number of ounces of gold to buy a brand-new car today as it did in the '60s, but it takes a different number of dollars to buy that same brand-new car. The dollars have depreciated. That is an important point, as you will see a little later on.

The second problem is that we entered a period of large deficit financing by the government. Year after year, we have had $20 to $30 to even $60 billion federal deficits; the Federal Government, in other words, has spent more money than it has taken in. That has, essentially, the same effect as an increase in the money supply; since we are spending dollars that we really don't have, we have to borrow and, later on, print more dollars to pay back what we owe.

This has led to the third, and most important, problem. Our national debt is now so large that interest payments alone on the debt in the next eighteen months, are going to add up to about $100 billion; this single expenditure, for interest on our national budget, will be the third largest item of expense! We now spend more for the interest on our national debt than we do on our Department of Agriculture, Veterans' Administration, all Presidential funds combined, our Department of Education, and any other three or four departments you would like to toss in for good measure.

Given these considerations, gold becomes "mouse-trapped". The increase in money supply through deficit spending, and, of course, the weakening of the dollar, makes people leery of holding onto dollars. They want to hold onto something of true value, like gold.

Gold will always represent true wealth. That is the key to the spectacular success in gold trading. That is also the reason why the price of gold should start coming down during the Reagan administration. If you continue to remember, and tell yourself, that gold represents true wealth, I think you are always going to be on the right side in these precious metal markets.

Gold is the one venerable storehouse of value that has stood the test of time from the dawn of creation; and it will continue being the storehouse of value. If you doubt that, simply check with your local historian or take a trip to your library and find out what has happened in other countries when they have started to go off gold or silver standards.

Whenever money has been backed by precious metals, governments, in an attempt to make themselves larger and more significant, have needed more money. To do that they depreciate the value of their currencies either by backing the currency with fewer ounces of precious metals, or simply offering paper money instead of gold-backed funds. Whenever this takes place, the price of gold soars and the value of the currency declines radically.

What Will Cause Gold to Fall

As people realize that the dollar is becoming weaker, they drive the price of gold sky-high. The mathematics of the equation alone will push currency down and gold up; but the emotional situation must also be taken into consideration. Investors, whether astute or not so astute, see the scarcity of gold and the weakness of the currency and rush in to purchase gold, or sell dollars, driving dollars lower and gold even higher.

But when a currency is as good as gold, or is backed by gold, the demand for gold drops about 80%. There is a very simple reason for this. There is no real use for gold, other than for some commercial value and jewelry. It is very hard to spend gold. You can't go into a restaurant and carve off a few slices of gold to pay for your meal. If the dollar is as good as gold, it's preferable to carry dollars around. After all, you can put a lot more dollars in your hip pocket and barter with them more easily than you can by weighing out pieces of gold; and if the dollar is backed by gold, or is as good as gold, then the paper fully represents the very storehouse of wealth.

I'm certain even the most adamant "gold bug" would agree with everything I've said up to this point. So now it's time for me to separate myself from the traditional "gold bugs," and tell you why I think we are going to see lower gold prices and higher U.S. dollar prices over the coming few years.

I believe it is possible for us to get out of the economic doldrums because our government is a democracy, not a totalitarian state. Other nations have been destroyed by debasing their currencies. The United States of America will go down in history as the only society to save itself, because, although we have debased our currency, and our system has gotten somewhat out-of-whack, we can change things because of the democratic process.

Why We Will Have a Gold-Backed Dollar Again

We are about to experience an evolutionary economic upswing. It will be brought about by President Ronald Reagan. My sources within the Reagan network of economic advisors strongly suggest that we will see, in the third year of President Reagan's first term, a return to the gold-backed dollar in this country.

That is, perhaps, the most important sentence of this book, because if we *do* back the dollar with gold, *and I do believe that's going to happen*, inflation will be halted instantaneously, the price of the dollar will come to a firm position and the price of gold will at the very least hold at a fixed level and stay pretty much in that stabilized price zone. If the dollar is as good as gold, there is simply no need to hold on to gold. The speculative surge will have been destroyed.

Ten years ago, people referred to gold as a "barbaric" metal; and the world's editorial writers were saying how horrible it would be if the dollar were backed with gold, how it would be unjust, unfair and against motherhood and applie pie as well.

But they have finally discovered what we have known all along: that the most barbaric thing one could do to society was to subject it to inflation rates of 18% to 20%. We have been subjected to those inflation rates; we have been subjected to the incredible decline of the U.S. dollar; and I believe we have learned our lesson. Certainly President Reagan knows of the relationship between gold and dollars. His economic advisors know of that relationship. His leading economic advisor, Arthur Laffer, is a great proponent of the gold-backed dollar.

When This Will Happen, and What Will Happen Then

I expect that we will see this done most likely in the third year of Reagan's first term; and gold will not be at a fixed price. If it is at a fixed price, we could still have some problems. The idea would be for the President simply to say that on Tuesday, the 19th day of the following month, at whatever price gold is trading at that point, we will use that price to back dollars. We certainly do not need a politician, an economist or a college professor to tell us where the price of gold should be: the price should be precisely where the market bids it to be. If the Reagan administration will be content with the prices determined in the free market and *then* convert the dollar, we will see an immediate halt to the major economic problems we have. I do believe that before the conversion of the dollar we are going to see the Reagan administration solve some of our economic problems. But the real turning point will be when gold, once again, becomes the standard. The Yankee dollar will once again become sound.

The Silver Bear

Silver has followed the price of gold pretty closely over the years, and I would expect that once we go to gold backing, the silver market will drop as well. My personal estimate is that markets exceed where they should go, based on the mathematics of the fundamental situation, by about 30%. There is at least that much emotional splurge or binge in markets at all times. So 30% of the price of silver or gold is due to the speculative excesses caused by the fear of the lessening of the dollar. You may want to use that 30% figure once you start hearing about backing the dollar with gold, and use that as an expectation of where gold and silver prices should top and bottom. But if the dollar, in fact, will be as good as gold, it will also be as good as silver, which is as good as gold; because silver is as good as gold, the price of silver should lose its glimmer as well.

Why the Government Should Buy Up Gold

The ideal situation would be for the United States government to place its own gold price above the market price. That way, people would turn their gold back into the United States government, and we could return all that beautiful, wonderful, splendid, delightful, delicious gold to Fort Knox and have more gold to back our dollars with.

I'd like to make a point about all the gold that the U.S. did sell. It should be a lesson to my generation, my children and my children's children, of how terribly inefficient political and economic forecasters can be. Can you imagine the absurdity of selling the most precious asset that our country has—its gold—at ridiculously low prices in an attempt to stabilize the dollar?

The last time people did anything as stupid was two centuries ago, when it was thought medically sound to take blood out of a person's body to make him stronger. Whoever came up with that idea must have been related to the idiot who came up with the idea that by selling gold one becomes financially stable. One becomes financially stable by putting more gold in the vaults, not by taking gold out of the vaults. Thus, if the government did offer an even higher price for gold than the market price, we would see an influx of gold into the treasury; and that would be good.

Whose Fault Is It Anyway?

It is interesting to look back at the last few years and see who has been blamed for inflation and other economic problems. At one point, President Nixon was blaming the speculators in the commodity markets for inflation. Then the blame shifted to the "gold bugs" and people who were holding onto precious metals. Other people have tried to pin the blame on unions who continually ask for more money to keep up with the increased cost of living, while still other parties try to blame it on business. We may have hit the very pinnacle of absurdity when President Jimmy Carter said the reason we're having so much inflation was because we were all using our BankAmericards too much. It's no wonder he was returned to the peanut farm. The lesson we have learned is that, in fact, some things *do* stay the same, that monetary values persist through history and the blame for lower dollar prices or for inflation falls only on the men who sell the storehouse of value behind our currency.

But equally fortunately, is that there seems to now be a collective realization in America of what we have done and correcting it. That is really the bottom line good news of this book. People have awakened to the reality that rocks are hard, water is wet and that budgets must be in balance, that the budget for the United States government is no different from the budget for any household in the country.

When Gold Will Lose Its Glitter

As I have mentioned, I look to the Reagan administration to back the dollar with gold in about the third year of President Reagan's term. I think that as it dawns on people that we are going back to the gold standard, we will see an overall downward slide in the market. Now, it may actually make the price of gold go up in the short run; but in any event, I would expect that the market itself will know this is about to take place, so you should watch what the market does six months prior to the time that we do convert to gold. If the market has reversed itself sharply to the up or down-side before the conversion takes place, I would look for a continuation of that trend.

There is a strong possibility that if the initial Reagan economic elixirs don't work we may move onto the gold standard before the three years are up, so you should be paying attention, as I am certain you already are, to inflation indexes, money supply figures, etc.; and if the tax cuts and productivity increase measures do not seem to be taking hold, then I would look for an even more rapid transition to the gold standard.

Just How Good Has Gold Been?

We've all heard stories about the tremendous fortunes that have been made buying gold and silver. We've even heard about the tremendous fortunes that have been lost in the silver market. I'd like to share with you some of what has taken place in the gold market. In January, 1981, spot gold has been selling for about $450.00 an ounce. One year previous spot gold was selling for about $600.00 an ounce. If we look back further, to, let us say, January 1979, we see gold was selling for approximately $250.00 an ounce, which means the price of gold has increased 100% in the last two years. If we look back yet another year, to January 1978, when gold was selling for approximately $175.00 an ounce, we come up with 214% gain. If we take the low at $200 an ounce in 1978, up to the all-time high in gold at $800.00, we will arrive with a 300% gain.

That should give you some parameters of the profit you could have made in gold if you had done precisely the right thing, by buying at an extremely low point and selling at an extremely high point. I don't know of anyone who did exactly that, and I doubt you or I would have done that; but that was the maximum opportunity. A more normal opportunity would have been, perhaps, a 100% profit, had you been fortunate enough to buy it at the right time and hold on to it. I should point out, however, that you may not have been that fortunate and you may have been a large purchaser of gold in January 1980, at the $800.00 level. If you bought it there and are currently holding onto it, you have suffered a loss of some 31% on your money; so gold has not really been a sure thing.

The Success of Stocks vs.
The Success of Gold

I have in front of me the net change in closing prices for the 1980 New York Stock Exchange. Just out of curiosity, I've taken the very first ten stocks in alphabetical order and have calculated their percentages of increase in the last 12 months. Keep in mind that gold was up 10% during that time period.

The first position was up 15%. The second position, AARS, was up 15%; the next position, ACF, was up 35%. The next position, AM International, was down 7%. The next position was down 23%. ARA was down 6%. The next position was ASA, a gold stock, which was up substantially, though gold itself was not up, which should tell you how ephemeral investing in gold and gold stocks can be. ASA was up a staggering 56%. ATO was up 50%. AVX was up 10%. Abbot Laboratories was up 37%. Even a random selection shows that there was much more money to be made on a percentage basis in the stock exchange than in gold. Out of curiosity, I started with all the stocks starting with the letter "O" (for Optimism). Again we can see that six out of the first ten stocks had gains similar to, or even greater than, what occurred in the gold market. As another test, I took all stocks starting with "L". Five of those first ten stocks showed gains more substantial than gold.

This is not a recommendation for any stocks, or for throwing darts to select your stocks, but it is an example of the type of gains that did occur in the stock market at a time the gold bugs were hoarding gold. It's evident they were doing the wrong thing. If you still have doubts, take a look at some of the more spectacular stocks I have not selected at random, like Burlington Northern, which was up some 128% for the year; CLC, which was up 25% for the year; Humana, which was up 130% for the year; Macom, which was up 190% for the year; N. MED. MENS, which was up 208% for the year; and on it goes. It's even more spectacular if you turn attention to the "over-the-counter" stocks, where you had gains in such stocks as TELCO, with a 145% gain; VRC INS, with a gain of 370%; SIEER RSH, with a 100% gain; and STSC, with a 188% gain.

Even the Mutual Funds did well in 1980, and most of them outsurpassed what the gold bugs were able to do with their buy-and-hold strategy in the gold market. Again, taking just the first ten listed Mutual Funds for 1980, we find that the first fund was unchanged for the year; the second fund, the Acorn Fund, was up approximately 15%; the ADV Fund was up 25%; A Future was up approximately 10%; a group, IAM Funds, was up almost 20%; and on it goes, as you can see.

One of the many adages of investing is that "the trend is your friend." What works, works; and the results of the stock market versus the gold market for 1980 show that there have been more spectacular successes trading stocks than trading gold; and even more spectacular successes for buying and holding stocks or Mutual Funds than buying and holding gold.

Gold Is Not "Old Faithful"

One of the leading contentions of the gold bugs is that you should buy gold and hold it forever. Some of the gold advisors have gone so far as to say, "Bury it in your backyard, put it in bank vaults, or hide it some place for when things do fall apart at the seams." The more intelligent gold bugs have tried to use a buy-and-hold strategy throughout the year, but I don't know of anyone who got his people out of the gold market at the top; most got their people out of the gold market after gold had peaked. In fact, some advised their clients to buy gold at, or very near, the top in the first part of the year or at the two tops that occurred later on in 1980. The trading strategy in the gold market has not been particularly profitable for those who have tried it.

For long term investors I think the lesson is clear. Gold is speculative; gold moves all over the board. Stocks are also speculative and move all over the board, but the net result over the last two years, shows that there have been more spectacular moves in stocks and real estate on a buy-and-hold basis than in gold, silver, or diamonds.

What works does work in the stock market. The mathematicians call it "relative strength", and their thesis is that you buy whatever stock has been going up the most and continue holding onto that stock. It has not been a bad selection technique, and under any "relative strength" measurements, you would have to rate gold as a very poor performer.

Why Diamonds May Not Be a Girl's Best Friend

Now that you've heard the bitter truth about gold, I'm afraid I've got to also tell you about the pitfalls of investing in diamonds. Before I begin, though, let me assure you that the case presented herein applies equally to silver.

I don't know how you feel about diamonds, but I happen to think they are absolutely beautiful. They are exquisite. They look particularly well on my wife's hand, and my wife and I do own several diamonds worth a substantial amount of money.

But we did not purchase them as an investment. We purchased them for their beauty. For that reason they have value to us. They do not have value to us on an investment basis, however.

There has been a tremendous diamond hype on the part of investment advisors over the last four years. The boiler-room operators have dragged out charts indicating why the price of diamonds has gone up in the past and why it will continue to rise in the future. The problem with those charts is that they reflect what has happened to diamonds on a retail level, not necessarily on a wholesale level. Any diamond you buy (unless you happen to be in the business) is going to be bought at some type of a retail level. If you buy it directly from your jeweler on Main Street in the city you live in, you are buying at the absolute end of the cycle. That means you were "the greater fool." You paid full retail. If you buy from a firm that is selling diamonds as an investment, you are again paying a retail price, perhaps not as great a retail price as in a jewelry store, so you are not quite as big a fool. But you are a fool nonetheless, because the diamond merchandisers have bought their diamonds, in turn, from someone else along the distribution channel.

This means that when you go to sell your diamonds, you

have two strikes against you. The first is the brokerage commissioner's sales charge. Those guys don't sit all day long calling you for the fun of it, or just to make certain that your money is invested wisely. They are doing it for a living. They make their money selling diamonds. So you have that expense to cover. Then you have to find someone who will buy your diamond at the price you paid for it or higher.

Are Diamonds Really Worth Anything?

But stop and think about it for a moment. Who is going to buy your diamond? What are you going to do, run an ad in the paper? Walk down Main Street, telling people you have a diamond for sale? And it means nothing to have your valuable diamond appraised. I have a diamond that I purchased for approximately $9,000, not at wholesale, but through a dealer in the trade, so I know he made a substantial profit for himself. I brought the diamond home and had it appraised at $17,000. But if you seriously think I can sell my $9,000 diamond for $17,00 all of a sudden, I wish you would write me a personal letter, because there is a bridge in Brooklyn you may also be interested in purchasing.

What I'm saying then, is that the appraised value, the market value, the retail value and wholesale value of diamonds are subject to a great many fluctuations, cuts, commissions, charges, loads, etc. The problem comes not from buying the diamond, but from trying to sell it later on. People who bought diamonds ten or fifteen years ago have an even greater problem: diamonds are cut differently now. Some of the old diamonds are very beautiful, and on that basis make a good investment for their beauty, but are no longer marketable, because cutting styles have changed and the stones may be worth only their initial purchase price.

What Sort of Commodity Is a Diamond?

If you are dealing in diamonds, I think you are dealing in trouble. Again, I ask you to stop and think about it for a moment. Let's say the world does fall apart; there are riots in the streets, shortages of food, and things are tough, to say the least. And you, with your pockets full of diamonds, are hungry or want a car, gasoline, shelter. If someone has one of those items, which at that point would be very scarce, how willing do you think he would be to part with his necessities in exchange for a pretty piece of stone?

It seems a little absurd, doesn't it, that someone is going to sell you food for their survival so they can have a diamond, when all they could do with it is go out and try to barter with someone else to try to get some more food for them to live on in exchange for the diamond that they get from you. That's getting right to the quick of the diamond and gold investment hype, but I think that's what we've got to do. Now you've got a picture of just what would take place and just how valuable, or, rather, valueless diamonds really are.

One leading authority on the diamond business suggests that the mark-up from the time a stone leaves the cutter to when it gets to the end purchaser, you or I, may be as much as 300%. The problem is, you don't know quite where you fall in line in that 300% cut. Most likely, you are buying at 75%— 100% above the cutter's cost; and the cutter isn't himself going to pay such a price for the stone.

Finally, let me say to you that if you are really sold on diamonds you should purchase them for the enjoyment they bring to you because of their beauty. You should be willing to hold onto the diamonds for at least ten to fifteen years, when the price of diamonds might have appreciated substantially enough that you can again find a market where they can be sold for a profit. I would also advise that you try to buy as large a diamond as possible and purchase the best quality of a diamond that you can. One thing for sure in purchasing diamonds, or anything of fine value, is that you want to get the very best; because that is the scarcest. If you do that you may not reap a spectacular gain for yourself during the 80's or 90's, but you will have a beautiful investment that, in time, should increase in value. On the other hand, cutting styles may change again, and if that happens, you should expect very little.

The problem, then, with investing in diamonds and gold is that you tie up investment capital that might be put to more spectacular use. Frankly, I'd rather make several hundred thousand dollars a year trading commodities, putting land deals together, and purchasing stock in expanding companies and then take my profits and buy my wife a diamond. I know a lot of investors, but I don't know any investors that have been able to make several hundred thousand dollars a year, year-in and year-out, buying and selling diamonds.

Summary

Let me again remind you how vitally important I believe it is for our dollar to be backed by gold. If we do not back the U.S. dollar with gold during the next four years, many of the prophecies in this book, especially the ones pertaining to gold, may not come about.

At some point, this country simply must get back to an understanding that dollars must represent true value or wealth. All true wealth comes, ultimately, from the ground or the oceans. A dollar could represent 50 bushels of wheat, an ounce of gold, ten cords of wood, or three pounds of beef. It doesn't matter; as long as there is a real representation of wealth, the dollar will be strong. The most convenient item to use, of course, is gold. It's small, it's storable, and there is a good market for it.

If the dollar is converted, I think that will make the big economic explosion for the early '80s; and what I've been saying will be on track; and you should treat the markets accordingly. By the same token, if we get conclusive evidence that we will not convert the dollar to gold, then you'll find me back on the bullish side of gold and the bearish side of the dollar. As it stands right now, I think the conversion is going to be the major economic surprise to the investment community, and this is why I see us losing the glitter for gold and gaining the glitter for America.

Perhaps the impact of having currencies backed by precious metals, or even agricultural products; something that, in fact, is true wealth, can best be seen in the following writings: "Blood running in the streets . . . lootings of shops and homes . . . credit ruined, strikes and unemployment . . . trade and distribution paralyzed . . . shortages of food . . . kidnappings for heavy ransoms . . . sexual perversion, drunkenness, lawlessness rampant . . . the wheels of government clogged, and we are descending into a valley of confusion and darkness . . . no day was ever more clouded than the present."

If that sounds to you like Harry Schultz, or another of the doomsday crowd, you might be relieved to know that these are the words of former President, George Washington, in a letter written ten years after he signed the Declaration of Independence. A year later, in a letter to General Henry Knox, Washington said, "If any person had told me there would have been such formidable rebellion as this, I would have thought him fit for a mad-house."

What was the problem Washington was talking about? Simply that caused by the Continental Dollar, which, wrote Washington's good friend, Peletiah Webster, "ceased to pass as currency, but was afterwards sold as speculation for 500/1,000 to 1.

On June 11, 1980, there was a meeting of the President's economic Advisory Board. Present were Milton Friedman, George Schultz, Alan Greenspan, William Simon, Arthur Burns, and other heavy hitters within the Republican economic circles. The discussion was on taxes, spending cuts, and, then, monetary policy.

After a good deal of discussion, USC economist, Art Laffer, gave a strong pitch, advocating that the dollar be backed with gold. There were some critical comments from around the table, as might be expected, especially from the previous "Establishment Economists."

Following the discussion, one voice spoke out, and said, "I don't know. I think Art's got a lot of credibility there. You know, never in the history of the planet has a nation ever survived without a convertible currency."

That was the voice of President Ronald Reagan.

3

Commodities: The Fastest Game in Town and the Best Investment for the '80s

Winner Take All:
The Commodities Market

The key to trading commodities is to constantly remember it is a "winner-take-all" game.

The economics of "winner take all" translates to a basic axiom: if you make money in the commodity market, you will make more money than you ever thought possible; if you lose money in the commodity market, chances are you are going to lose all of the money or at least a substantial part of what you put up. Seldom, if ever, is there an average performance from a commodity trader. Most often there are spectacular failures and successes; precious few commodity traders remain in the middle.

To give just one example of how spectacularly successful trading commodities can be, I recall in the late 1973 market, one person to whom I was giving commodity advice started with about $3,500 and ran his nest egg to almost $65,00 in a period of less than four months. Even more recently, in the summer of 1980, I gave some commodity advice to an attorney friend of mine who started in the markets with a mere $2,500. By the end of 1980, the $2,500 had grown to slightly over $17,000, netting him what he thought was an incredible 580% gain in less than six months.

Big Losses, Big Gains

I'm certain he had visions of chucking the law books out the window and retiring early. Naturally, I'd like to think it was my ability to forecast the markets that accounted for the substantial gain; it was more likely a combination of my talents and some very good and fortunate markets moving in our favor.

I say that because I've seen equally spectacular results on the down-side. All we commodity advisors have given people trade suggestions that have almost wiped them out financially.

In 1980, at least three Commodity Mutual Funds closed down because the fund managers lost most—if not all—of the fund's money. When you consider that these funds, on the average, ran from $2 to $10 million, you get better perspective on the dangers and potential devastations of trading commodities.

But there is always the other side of the coin; it *is* possible to reap consistently substantial rewards by trading commodities. I myself have probably averaged somewhere in the area of 500% to 600% profits each and every year since I first began trading commodities in 1969. During any given time period I may well have been down substantially, but fortunately by year's end things worked back in my favor.

So, if you are looking for action, are willing to take the risks and suffer the sleepless nights that a 600% to 1,000% return on your money each year can produce, then commodity trading is indeed for you. I hope I have put the fear of God in you about commodities, because that is what you need to have when trading them. Without the fear of God, you're going to fall asleep at the wheel and have a crack-up somewhere along the freeway of commodity trading. There are no slow lanes in this business, only fast lanes; and there are pot-holes, icy corners and road blocks that you need to be aware of.

Why Commodities Are the Best Investment of the '80s

However, I also think that it is easier to trade commodities than virtually any other investment opportunity not only because the reward potential is so great, but because the data, or input, for the commodity markets is cleaner, clearer and more honest than is data on investing in gold, diamonds, real estate or stocks.

Consider, if you will, a company that goes public and offers their stock on the open market. It issues stock and raises the money it needs for the corporation. It takes that money and does whatever it wants with it. The stock then continues fluctuating on the open market, and except for, perhaps, personal stockholders within the company, the company usually never has any direct involvement in the price fluctuations after that point. It isn't in on the profits, nor does it suffer the losses. The investor gets a piece of paper that represents a certificate of so many shares in the corporation.

I'd like to suggest to you that there is absolutely no one in the entire universe that *needs* a share in a company. After all, a share is just that—a piece of paper. And there is no use for the certificate. You can hang it on your wall and it may look pretty there, or perhaps you can get a loan against it, but it has no intrinsic value. It is simply a piece of paper, representing a concept; and you bought that concept because you believed the corporation was going to make more money in the future. But there is no true supply or demand for stock certificates. It is based on the abstract possibility that you can buy and sell it to someone else at a higher price later on.

Contrast that, if you will, with what takes place in the commodity market. There is a very real need for wheat, corn, soybeans, gold, silver, platinum, copper, soybean oil, plywood, lumber, cotton, cocoa and sugar. These are real items, necessary every day of the year. Thus, there are real-world supply/demand factors affecting the commodity market that simply do not have an effect on most investment opportunities. Even in real estate it is difficult to find a real supply/demand factor. In the last fifteen years most real estate has been bought not because people have needed to move into new areas or purchase new lands, but because they believe they can sell the land to someone else later on at a higher price. That's known as the "greater fool" theory: I may be a fool for buying it at this price, but I'm going to find an even greater fool to unload this stuff on later. That may be true; but because it is based on the "greater fool" theory we do not have reliable supply/demand data to base our investment decisions upon. That's the advantage of trading commodities. We have crop reports that tell us what the approximate size a crop will be; we can learn the production rates of gold or silver; we can find out how many cattle or hogs have been slaughtered or are still in the pens.

We also know what sort of demand there will be for these items, based on known consumer behavior patterns. Thus, we can establish equations that deal with true value. There are perhaps as many evaluations of what price should be as there are commodity traders, but we at least have parameters to work with here. Basically, we know that the end result—the price of a commodity—is going to be impacted by the seasonal influence, or the seasonality of price action itself; by the supply/demand equation (supply and demand account for perhaps 70% of price action); by a weighing factor of the current inflation rate; and, finally, by the emotions of commodity investors and traders.

The "Commercials"

Best yet for the average commodity trader is that there are substantial interests in the commodity markets, on the part of those whose business depends on their forecasting correctly current commodity trends. These people are good at it not only because they study it a substantial amount of the time, but because they are themselves involved in establishing the true supply/demand factors.

These are the people I have labeled "the Commercials," because they use the commodity product for commercial purposes. Some examples of "Commercials" in the grain markets are Continental Grain, Cargill, General Mills, Pillsbury, the large baking companies throughout America, and others.

These "Commercials" account for perhaps as much as 70% of the true volume of the commodity markets. Therefore, if we can find out what these people are doing by tracking their market activities, we should, in theory, have a pretty good idea of the overall trends of the market. I mean, after all, if the "big boys" have been buying wheat and corn, it's going to be a safe bet that that is what *you* should be doing as well. Thus, a substantial part of commodity analysis should focus on what the astute, informed players of the game are doing. It may not be unusual, for example, for one of these commercial users to move car loads of wheat from Chicago to Minneapolis or Kansas City to Chicago so as to pick up a nickle a bushel on the price. That's why I've always said, "The boys with the trains are the ones who have the brains." They have proven, by amassing large amounts of capital, that they usually know what's taking place in the commodity market. Thus, a good deal of my analysis focuses on what these commercial users are doing. I then attempt to duplicate their market performance.

Real Supply/Demand and "the Big Boys"

Bernard Baruch, who has been called the most brilliant speculator and investor in the history of the world, left a legacy of not only social comment, but market commentary as well. He said, "Nothing—may I repeat—nothing, has cost this country and the rest of the world more . . . than the failure to grasp the enormous difference in the workings of supply and demand. The law of supply and demand . . . this is the most basic of all economic laws. The workings of supply and demand never stop. They form an endless process of adjustment, which is always going on." I have found Baruch's beliefs on the impact of supply and demand to be all-important; and I know no better way of monitoring supply/demand than following the people who follow supply/demand most closely. They have access to so much more information that I find it more valuable to concentrate my energies and time riding on their coattails than to do all of the leg work myself.

After all, Hershey may have as many as 20 analysts projecting the potential price for cocoa; Englehard Minerals has another 20 or 50 analysts working on the price of gold and silver; Swift and Company has 30 meat analysts; and Pillsbury has 20 or 30 grain analysts. I simply don't have the resources or the time to study the fundamentals of each and every market. But I do have the resources and time to follow the players in the individual markets who have already done their own homework.

How to Determine What the Commercial Interests Are Doing

In my search for Nirvana in the commodity markets, I have stumbled across four usually reliable measures of what the "big boys" are doing in the market place. Three of them pertain specifically to monitoring what the large interests are doing. You have to remember that the large interests got so large because they were the smartest players in the game; and even though they will be wrong from time to time, over any given time span they should be correct.

Chart 2
1970 Open Interest for Plywood

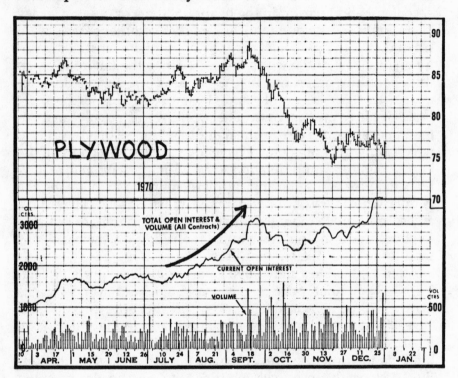

We can see how large an impact these interests have on the markets by measuring what we in the commodity market call "Open Interest." Open Interest represents the net number of positions, long and short, in a commodity. In Chart 2, above, the Open Interest line is the dark line at the bottom that moves up and down along the chart. Traditional analysis of Open

Interest has resulted in a great fallacy. The fallacy has been that when Open Interest declines, price should also decline.

Chart 3
Basic Open Interest Signals

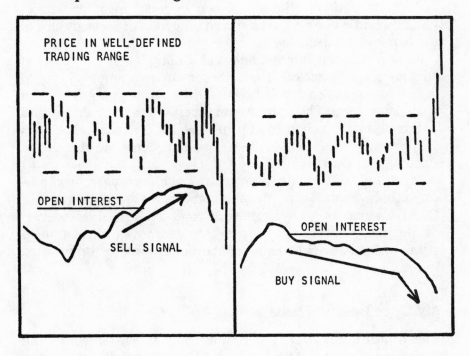

Open Interest and Commercial Activity

I believe I established in my first commodity book, *How I Made One Million Dollars Trading Commodities Last Year* (1973) that that is a fallacy; in fact, what Open Interest represents is the *commercial* activity, and, if monitored and understood correctly, it can help one to forecast substantial commodity market moves.

The thing one needs to remember in evaluating the Open Interest is that the large commercial users account for as much as 70% of market volume or Open Interest. In other words, what that little line on the chart is a reflection of the activities of the commercial users.

Now, the Open Interest line will decline if, *and only if, short sales are being liquidated.* The only reason a commercial would liquidate a short sale is if he envisions prices going higher at some later point. The only reason Open Interest would expand or increase on the chart (go up-hill), would be *because short sales are increasing.* This would be a sign that someone thinks the price will go down.

My study of the markets over the last eleven years has indicated that we cannot simply take every increase and decrease in Open Interest as an indication or forecasting tool. However, during those times when Open Interest moves in relation to price, we *can* predict some substantial upward or downward move.

My Open Interest Thesis

The original thesis on Open Interest was presented to the American commodity trader in my "Million Dollar" commodity trading book. Since then (1973), the book has stood the test of time and has become a major forecasting tool used by many commodity traders throughout the world.

The basic assumption of my Open Interest technique is that if you are in an over-all bullish market trend (prices have been rising), and then go into a trading range where prices essentially move sideways for a period of time, while at the same time Open Interest declines, we can then assume that the commercial interest are liquidating their short sales. Why? Because they believe the up-trend that took place prior to the sideways move of the market should be resumed.

The reverse would indicate that the Commercials are expecting lower commodity prices. That would mean you would need

Chart 4
Signals for Cotton in May, 1980

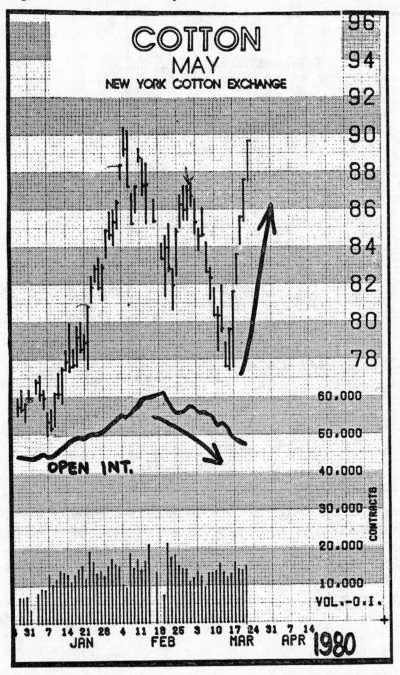

Chart 5
Signals for Copper in December, 1971

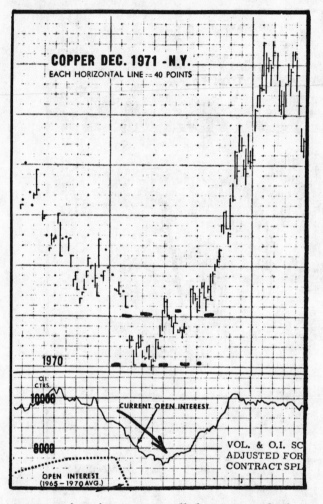

to see prices in an over-all down-trend, then see them moving sideways at the same time as Open Interest expands or increases substantially. That would indicate that the Commercials are adding to their short sales in the market in the belief that there is a decline to come.

So that you might see the validity of my Open Interest

theory, I have charts of the model as it should appear, in theory. Charts 4 and 5 illustrate the reliability of my Open Interest theory. Pay particular attention, if you will, to the cotton open-interest signals chart of March 1980. You should, of course, realize that this theory works not only for edible commodities, such as meats and grains, but also for the more utilitarian commodities, such as cotton, platinum, gold and silver.

The *Commitment of Large Traders*

Another way of monitoring what the informed people are doing in the commodity market is provided for us on a monthly basis by the United States Department of Agriculture through their publication, the *Commitment of Large Traders*. The *Commitment of Large Traders* shows what the "big boys" are doing as opposed to what the little people are doing in the commodity market. Year in and year out I have noticed that the Large Traders tend to do the right thing more often than the Small Traders. You can get this report by writing the United States Department of Agriculture, 141 West Jackson Street, Chicago, Illinois, 60603; or it may be monitored in several of the chart services, such as Commodity Research's excellent chart service: 1 Liberty Plaza, New York City, N.Y., 10006.

One of the problems with this information is that it is released on a monthly basis, and thus, is somewhat delayed. Nonetheless, it is significant enough for the commodity trader or investor to check it and see whether he is on the side of the Large Trader or the Small Trader. You should also notice the changes that are taking place: are the Large Traders and Commercials decreasing their long positions or increasing their long positions? The question is whether the commitment of the Large Trader is increasing or decreasing. The answer to that will give you significant forecasting insight.

The third way to monitor the activity of the Commercials is to observe the price fluctuation of the same commodities in different months.

The Secret to Commodity Market Premiums

Perhaps as much as 90% of the time, the more distant commodity contracts will sell for more money than the nearby contracts. As this is written in December of 1980, January and March contracts in soybeans are selling for less money than the distant contracts in August or November. There is a very good reason for this: time. As we all know, time is money; and the person who is going to deliver soybeans or gold in November—versus delivering in March—has more time to pay. That means added interest, storage charges, insurance, handling fees, etc. That's why it is typical for the more distant months to trade at a higher price than the nearby months.

At times, however, there is an inversion of this relationship, and the nearby commodity contracts sell for more money than the distant commodity contracts. That presents the investor with an outstanding Commercial Opportunity for a substantial bull market.

To my way of thinking there is one, and only one, reason why the nearby contracts would sell for more money than the distant contracts. Somebody wants them so badly that he is willing to pay a premium to get the commodity in their hands right now . . . today!

I don't believe the small speculators who walk in off the street and start trading commodities is willing to bid the commodity to a premium, simply because there are not enough of them and they don't control or have enough influence in the markets to do that. What drives these markets to premium prices is the fact that the commercial users, who do account for approximately 70% of the volume, want the commodities and are willing to pay the inverted premium price for them.

How to Find "The Bulls"

Thus, we have a third excellent tool that tells us what markets the Commercials are most concerned about and where we can be bullish. Simply by checking the *Wall Street Journal* or any other listing of commodity prices we can determine the commodities that have been bid the premiums.

The fact that the commodity is at a premium is a "green

light" sign you should use to consider trading that commodity from the long side. Additionally, you should watch these premium spreads to see when they change from the normal condition of nearby contracts selling for *less than* the distants to a premium market with the nearby selling for *more than* the distants. It is this relationship, or change, that is significant; and when a premium starts "coming on" . . . developing . . . you are alerted to the possibility of a substantial commercial bull market taking place.

Beware, however, the difference between a commercial bull market and a speculative bull market.

Gold has never gone into a premium in its entire bull market, as you can see from the long term chart on gold. It oscillates all over the place. It's had huge run-ups and equally spectacular smashes. This is characteristic of a speculative bull market; it is not "tight," generally because there is no true commercial demand for the product.

Contrast that, if you will, with the commercial bull markets that have taken place in cocoa, coffee and soybeans. Those markets were very tight, the pull-backs were limited and it was only when the bull market was all over that you got into the wild gyrations. All of these markets, sugar, coffee, cocoa, and soybeans were forecast well in advance because the premiums developing on nearby contracts raised selling prices to levels above those of distant months.

Seasonal Commodity Trading

There are two other factors that I would like to touch on briefly that may help the novice commodity trader. The first is that there is a strong seasonal influence on commodity prices; they rally at one time of the year and decline at another. This will, obviously, differ from one commodity to another: the time wheat is harvested is different from the time the cocoa crop is brought in. Building starts usually speed up in the spring of the year, and therefore lumber prices rise in the spring; but once housing construction begins, lumber prices start coming down. So that you might have a feel for the seasonal influences, I have included Chart 6 showing what the seasonal influences have been for the majority of actively traded commodities over the last 20 years. There has been a great deal of other work done on seasonal factors in the commodity market. I would suggest perhaps reading my book, *Sure Thing Commodity Trading—How Seasonal Factors Influence Commodity Prices*, available from Windsor Books, P.O. Box 280, Brightwater, New York, 11718; or *Profits Through Seasonal Trading*, by Jack Grushcow and Courtney Smith, available from Ronald Press, New York, New York.

Both these books will point out to you what the seasonal influences are and when you should, based on seasonal factors, expect market rallies or declines in individual commodities.

Commodity Contrariness

Finally, I think it is profitable to pay attention to "contrary opinion." If you ever get the time, I would suggest you read *Extraordinary Popular Delusions and The Madness of the Crowds*, by Charles MacKay, an illuminating book that covers the extraordinary swings in human emotions, from Tulipomania to stock speculations. MacKay has documented, perhaps as no one else ever has, how the majority of the people are wrong the majority of the time. As Bernard Baruch famously said, he, Baruch, ". . . always bought [his] straw hats in the winter."

I touched on this earlier: we are fortunate in that there are several people who rate the percentage of bullish and bearish professional commodity investors and advisory services. The service I follow is Market Vane, Pasadena, CA.: They issue on a weekly basis a percentage of advisory services that are bullish on a commodity.

History shows that when 80% or more of the investment advisors are bullish on a commodity, it may be in the area of a major top. By the same token, when the number of bullish investment advisors is 30% or less, you can expect that the commodity is in the general area of a major market low.

Well, there you have it! Some of the best tools of my trade have been presented to you in this chapter. It's my belief that if someone does take the time to study and understand the commodity markets, he has a good probability either of making a career out of trading the markets or at least a very nice, and in some cases, a substantial, second income. I think this is going

Chart 6
Seasonal Trading for Various Commodities

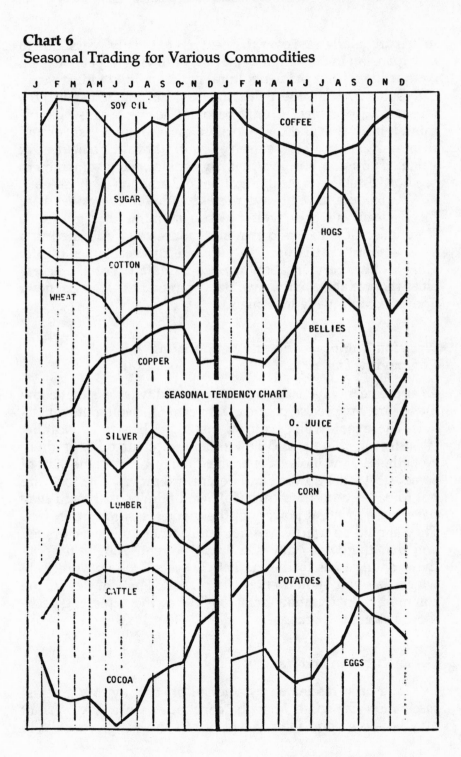

to be particularly true over the next ten to twenty years, due to an expansion in consumer demands, and what appears to be a contraction within the agricultural or commodity industry.

Despite what all the gold-bugs say and regardless of how scarce gold becomes, it only becomes scarce because people think it has value and they stock up on it. But gold, silver and diamonds, in and of themselves, don't have a great deal of value. If you don't believe that, try cooking them sometime to see how palatable a meal of gold and diamonds is. It isn't.

What people have always needed and will always need are food, water, air and shelter. Keep in mind that gold is a storehouse of value, and that storehouse can be likened to a bank account that is used to purchase the necessities of life. Gold is only a condensation of, or representation of, the necessities that we all have to have. But commodities we need, now. They are continually in demand.

Precision Timing for Entering and Exiting Commodity Trades

Over the years I have developed and used two tools that allow me to time my precise points of entry into the commodity markets. These tools will, of course, sometimes be wrong. Nothing is perfect in this up-and-down game of commodity trading. Nonetheless, the tools have enabled me to get in at the start of some substantial upward and downward moves. The tools are not to be used on their own, followed blindly as though they have some mystical powers in the market; far from it, in fact. They should be used when, and only when, other factors tell you that the commodity should be bought. *Then* you apply these timing tools to the market. They will tell you precisely which day you should enter the market. First, however, the commodity in question must have met the screening techniques I've just discussed.

Commodity Yin and Yang

I've long been fascinated by oriental philosophy. My greatest fascination has come from the concept of yin and yang, not only because I find the concept of yin and yang operative in daily activity but also because it seems to have a strong impact on the market. The original, millenia-old concept is simply that there are two forces in the world, by which everything may be defined. These forces are known as "yin" and "yang." Just as yin is about to overtake yang, yang gathers strength and begins to dominate yin. Then, just as yang is about to conquer yin, again the energy forces switch and yin once more develops its strength. And so it goes, an unending battle of good and evil, white and black, hot and cold, or simply: the markets over-bought and over-sold. My observation of market action shows that there is a similar imbalance of price action working at all times in the market place.

How to Tell When a Market Is Over-Sold

Enough about concepts and abstracts. Here is how I mathematically identify an over-bought or over-sold market. I have constructed an index, which I refer to as "Percent of R," or, simply, "Percent R." This index is a simple measure of where today's closing price fits within the total range of the last ten days. To arrive at the index, I take the highest intra-day high for the last ten days and the lowest intra-day low for the last ten days. This makes a band. I then look at where today's closing price fits within the band.

To do this, you subtract the low price of the last ten days from the high price of the last ten days. We call that figure the "range." Next, subtract today's closing price from the high of the last ten days. We'll call this the "change." Then, divide the "change" by the "range." You will arrive at the percentage of today's closing level to the total ten-day range. If, let's say, the highest high of the last ten days has been 86.50, and the lowest low of the last ten days has been 75.30, the "range" would be 11.20. If today's closing price is 76.10, you would subtract 76.10 from the high of 86.50, leaving a net value of 10.40. You then divide this "change" by the "range," giving us a percentage of .9%. This per cent figure is then plotted on a daily basis, underneath the general price action. As you can see from charts 6 and 7, when the index gets into the area below 10%, we are usually close to a market bottom, and when it gets into the area above 90%, we are usually close to, or at, a market top.

Chart 7
"Percent R" Indicator for Copper in March, 1974

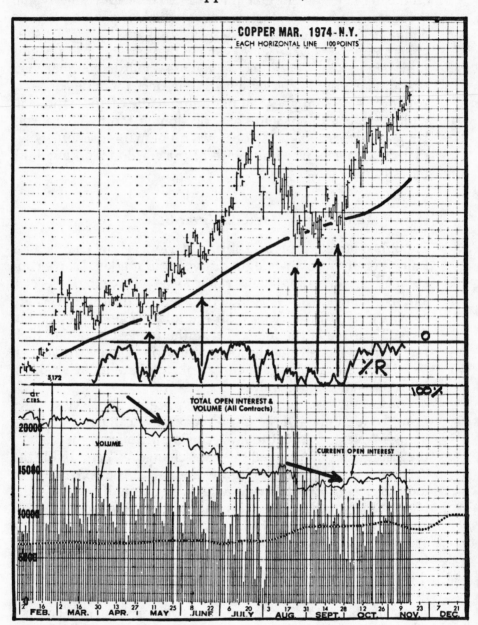

Chart 8
"Percent R" Indicator for Plywood, January, 1973

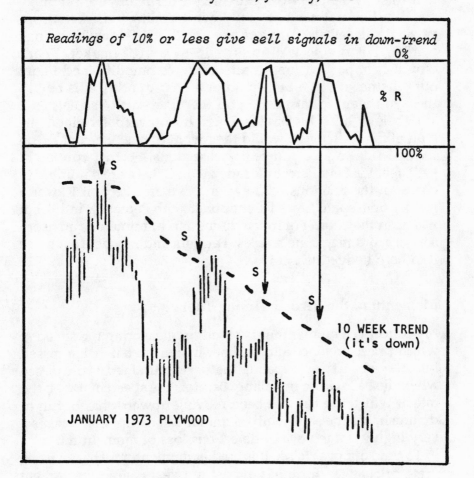

Readings of 10% or less give sell signals in down-trend

0%

% R

100%

S

S

S

S

10 WEEK TREND
(it's down)

JANUARY 1973 PLYWOOD

The most important thing I can tell you about the index is that the buy signals work extremely well in an "up-trending" market, but not well in a "down-trending" market. Conversely, the sell signals work very well in a "down-trending" market, but not so well in an "up-trending" market. That's why it is important first to screen the commodity, and figure out whether it's in a bull-trend or a bear-trend. If it is bullish then you want to take action on the "Percent R" signals as it falls below 90%, by buying long. If you've determined the market is bearish, you would then want to use "Percent R" on the sell-side to give you selling directions. So that you might get a feel for how Percent R Index works, here are a number of charts of the relationship between price and Percent R over a goodly time span. Since I went public with Percent R in 1973, it has been the subject of much discussion in numerous advisory services and magazine articles. Farmers and ranchers even use it to help hedge their crops.

Momentum: the Second Timing Tool

My concept of momentum is based on measuring the speed at which prices advance and decline. Imagine a ball being tossed into the air. At some point, the very untrained eye can see when the ball will begin falling, because the speed of travel, the rate at which the ball has been moving upward, has begun to diminish. It's the same with commodities, except that it takes a very highly trained eye to detect *this* loss of momentum.

To train our eyes to see this market momentum, I began using "rate of change" formulas almost ten years ago. One can get very complicated mathematically with these formulas. I have preferred to keep all of my mathematical work simple; simple enough that even a child can do it. The concept I'm about to describe can be followed on a daily basis, and is extremely simple. All you have to do is take the difference between the closing price today and the closing price of the commodity twenty-five days ago. That's all there is to it.

As an example: if the price of Pork Bellies closed at 65.30 twenty-five days ago, and today closed at 75.95, you would subtract the two numbers and find a positive value of 10.65.

That is the amount of change from the price twenty-five trading sessions ago to today's price. You would then do the same for the market tomorrow, and continue on. You then plot these numbers chronologically above or below a zero line on a graph with an appropriate scale. You connect the dots to form a solid line, and you will get an oscillator, a rate of change index that will peak and trough with commodity prices. It shows you the true reflection of momentum in the marketplace.

Peaks, Valleys, and Rallies

There are several ways one can go about using this momentum indicator to time your trades. When the momentum has started to peak out, as the charts show, commodity prices usually *then* follow and start moving down. This is the beauty of momentum. Momentum peaks and troughs occur in *advance* of price action. Hence, you can use trend-line analysis on momentum to forecast what will happen to the price of a certain commodity.

A second way you can use the momentum index is to aid in identifying the more important commodity tops and bottoms. This situation develops by means of *divergence;* I've marked on the charts several examples where commodity prices have gone higher on consecutive rallies, *while* the momentum is dropping. Instead of making new highs, each high on the momentum line is lower than the previous high, whereas the stock prices have gone higher. That is one indication that the momentum has totally run out of the market, and the market should have an important decline.

The reverse is equally true. Many substantial markets have fallen to consistent new lows at the same time that the momentum line is "walking up-hill." That action usually signifies that the market's downward move is all over and a rally of some magnitude is in the offing.

The Impact of the News on Commodity Prices

Ninety-nine percent of the commodity traders I know are glued to news sources and information throughout market sessions. However, they never know what to do with the news once they get the reports.

As I see it, commodity news is meaningless in and of itself. The fact that there has been a crop failure or a blight means absolutely nothing on its own. How the market *responds* to the news, however, is very important. In 1973, for example, the copper market hit an ultimate low, and it was announced that a large quantity of copper was to be placed for sale on the market. This should have caused a crash. Instead, prices did not crash, but barely declined, and—over the next few sessions—started advancing. The upward movement was staggering.

The message was clear. The market was in very strong hands. When the market *should* do something, and does *not* do it, that gives you a tremendous insight into the workings of the market.

Many people are convinced they should hold onto stock and commodity holdings because they hear very encouraging news about their positions. Instead of listening to the news, what they should do is notice what happens to the price after the news breaks. If the optimistic news is met by an equally optimistic rise in prices, you should continue holding your position. But if prices do not respond to the optimism and, instead, start moving sideways and down, then the market is telling you that the big players have known the news for a while, and it's most likely a good time for you to take action. We don't ring any bells in the market, but if you observe the response of price to news carefully, and when what should happen doesn't, you can hear the chimes begin to ring in your experienced ears.

The Great Silver Secret Revealed

I've been chided a good deal, from time to time, about a chapter in my first book on commodities in which I claimed there seemed to be some relationship between *a full moon* and commodity prices. I was not the first to make this observation. It's been made repeatedly over the years, but I was the first one to announce that it appeared that there was some type of relationship between new-moons and full-moons and the *price* of silver! Quickly following my research discoveries, several magazine articles appeared, vindicating the thesis.

The thesis is that silver tends to rally at the time of a full-moon and tends to decline at the time of a new-moon. Don't ask me why, and please believe me when I tell you I don't know anything about astrology. All I really know about is markets, and how they respond to things. If one had bought and sold silver in 1980 based on the "full-moon theory," the profit would have been astounding. There were almost $100,000 in profits had one acted on all of the indications that we first wrote about in 1973!

Do take all this about trading the markets on a full-moon with a grain of salt. My main reason for drawing it to your attention is that it is an interesting phenomenon that does seem to have some impact on commodity prices.

Creating New Wealth

If you take time to study the increases and decreases in population *vs.* the demise of the family farm and the agricultural problems we have been experiencing, I think it becomes apparent that we are going to have some food shortages over the next fifteen years. Frankly, I don't think these will be extreme shortages, but still the price of food is going to rise. For a good deal of time, both political parties have neglected the agricultural and agrarian interests in society in favor of votes in the city. They've done everything they can to keep food prices down so the inflation indexes won't look too severe and so they can stay in office. But we are reaching the pinnacle of this movement, and you are now going to see a return to the understanding that most true wealth comes from the farming or mining communities in this country. After all, by writing this book, I have not *produced* any new wealth. All I have been able to do is place words on sheets of paper; but it has not brought into existence new wealth for any person.

The same is true of lawyers, doctors and almost everyone in our society. We move pieces of paper and dollars around, from someone else's pocket to our own. The *creation* of new wealth comes from the land or from the oceans; it comes from timber,

mining, husbandry, food products or fibers. One of the underlying reasons for this is that there is no debit. Mother Nature
simply provides these things for us, if we are willing to invest
some time and elbow-grease in their development. But as the
transaction is completed, as the corn or wheat is harvested or
the animals brought to slaughter, there is no debit from Mother
Nature. It's strictly a credit-side transaction, whence comes
most of the world's wealth.

I will be looking, then, for some substantial moves in the
commodity markets over the next few years, and will be paying
very close attention to the development of premium situations
in individual commodities, as well as the Open Interest, to see
what the Commercials are doing.

Other Ways You Can Play the Commodity Market without Quite as Much Risk

There should be some other considerations about participating
in the commodity market boom—and make no mistake, it *has*
been a boom. There are more people now actively trading
commodities than there are people trading stocks. There are
ways of participating in this boom that do not entail quite so
much risk, too. One of those would be to buy farm land, which
is certainly going to go up in value compared to inner-city
property.

Farm land will go up in value for two reasons. First of all, it is
production land, and can be used for profitable business purposes, especially if you consider that we will see higher agricultural prices through the remaining part of this century. Second,
much of the development that's going to be taking place will be
expansionary. Those new lands which will be sought will be
farm land properties near cities. As cities expand they swallow
up nearby farm land, and at substantially higher prices than the
farm land was purchased for agricultural purposes.

You may also want to consider Commodity Mutual Funds.
Though their record has not been too spectacular, there have
been some good ones. But if I were you, I would try to find out
as much as I could about the commodity markets by yourself
and trade them accordingly.

Chart 9
Copper Computerized Track Record

```
COPPER   731001/801201
GROSS P/L               57091.16
TOTAL PROFIT            93732.02
AVE PROFIT                876.00
TOTAL LOSS            -36640.85
AVE LOSS                -373.89
AVE PROF / AVE LOSS        2.34
% RETURN ON MARGIN      1139.27
MAX UNREAL PROF         13155.41
MAX    REAL PROF        12289.59
MAX UNREAL LOSS        -4236.05
MAX    REAL LOSS       -1596.55
TOTAL # TRADES              205
# PROF TRADES               107
# LOSS TRADES                98
% OF TRADES PROF          52.20
TOT # DAYS IN POS          1566
# DAYS IN PROF POS         1152
# DAYS IN LOSS POS          414
AVE # DAYS IN POS             8
AVE # DAYS IN + POS          11
AVE # DAYS IN - POS           4
MAX # LOSSES IN A ROW         6
WRST RUN IN A + TRDE   -4236.05
MIN EQTY IN SPAN       -1265.74
MAX EQTY LOSS IN SPAN   5888.35
STDEV OF LOSS TRADES      293.72
COMMISSION                 43.20
MARGIN                    800.00
VALUE OF 1 UNIT MOVE      250.00
```

Commodity Systems

There are several commodity systems around. Over the years some of these have come up with mechanical ways of trading

Chart 10
Pork-belly Computerized Track Record

```
FZPK       700105/800801
GROSS P/L              95099.69
TOTAL PROFIT          227005.84
AVE PROFIT              1055.84
TOTAL LOSS           -131906.16
AVE LOSS                -527.62
AVE PROF / AVE LOSS        2.00
% RETURN ON MARGIN       634.00
MAX UNREAL PROF         8289.09
MAX   REAL PROF         7686.89
MAX UNREAL LOSS        -1610.27
MAX   REAL LOSS        -1610.27
TOTAL # TRADES             465
# PROF TRADES              215
# LOSS TRADES              250
% OF TRADES PROF         46.24
TOT # DAYS IN POS         2500
# DAYS IN PROF POS        1850
# DAYS IN LOSS POS         650
AVE # DAYS IN POS            5
AVE # DAYS IN + POS          9
AVE # DAYS IN - POS          3
MAX # LOSSES IN A ROW        6
WRST RUN IN A + TRDE     -984.50
MIN EQTY IN SPAN        -2916.69
MAX EQTY LOSS IN SPAN    6267.34
STDEV OF LOSS TRADES      303.76
COMMISSION                 54.00
MARGIN                   1500.00
VALUE OF 1 UNIT MOVE      380.00
```

the market, wherein one knows what his potential risks and rewards are and what type of approximate return he can expect.

In charts 9 and 10 I show what follows from a trading method I developed both for copper and pork bellies. Notice that in the years between 1973 to 1980 this particular commodity system took $46,722 in profits out of trading copper. The maximum loss at any one time was $5,888. So, I received almost ten times as much money in reward as I did in the losses I suffered. Additionally, only 51.71% of the trades were correct trades; which proves that the old adage, "You don't have to be right very often in the commodity markets," is true. In fact, most people are right 40% of the time and wrong 60% of the time; but as the profits are larger than the losses, it turns out to be a worthwhile venture. Notice in the case of the copper records the average profit was $766, and the average loss was $349.

The same system, when applied to the more volatile pork bellies market, has shown some $97,688 in profits, with an average profit of $1,000.53, and an average loss of $521. It was correct only 46% of the time; yet the maximum equity loss experienced at any one time was only $6,804—certainly not a bad risk when you consider the $97,000 reward. This was over a ten-year period, 1970–1980.

If you have a mathematical or mechanical mind, and have the discipline to follow a particular style or method, it may serve you well to find one of the better commodity systems or commodity trading methods. Simply apply that on a mechanical, by-rote, basis. If you do that, you may be very surprised at how profitable and easy commodity-trading can be.

How to Find Out More About Trading Commodities

There are several good commodity advisory services that you should get in touch with to learn more about commodity-trading and the different techniques people use. I would suggest that you read several books, including my own. *How I Made One Million Dollars Trading Commodities Last Year*, and *How Seasonal Factors Influence Commodities*, available from Windsor Books; as well as *Techniques of The Professional Commodity Analyst*, available from the Commodity Research Bureau, 1 Liberty Plaza, New York City, New York; *The Professional Commod-*

ity Trader, by Stanley Kroll, Harper & Row, 10 East 53rd Street, New York City, New York, 10022.

If this chapter has whetted your appetite, to find out more about the commodity market you should make a quick trip to your local brokerage firm. Stay with the major ones, like Merrill-Lynch, Shearson, Hayden, Stone, E.F. Hutton, etc. and ask them for as much information as they can give you on trading commodities. Almost all brokerage firms have some introductory material that will explain the jargon of trading commodities to you.

Further, the cost of entry is lower in commodity-trading than in anything I can think of. Commissions range from .2% to .4%; stock commissions, by contrast, usually average almost 1% on a trade. The margin usually required for purchasing commodities is 5% to 10%, compared to stock trading at 50% to 80%, or owning your own business at 70% to 100%. There is also no cost for the margin. In other words, you don't have to pay for the 90% of the money that you don't put up, as you are buying an option, not borrowing money for the transaction. If you buy stocks on margin, you have to make, currently, almost 15% interest payments. The same thing happens if you buy bonds.

Emotional Impact on the Commodity Market

If you take the plunge and start trading commodities, you will find yourself propelled between two emotional forces: greed and fear. Greed will drive you to hold onto your positions in hopes of higher profits. Fear will make you want to get out of the positions, because you may become afraid they are going to slip and you are going to lose some of the money that you had made or lose the money you started trading with. I advise that commodity trading be done only by people who have a very clear understanding of their emotions.

Abraham Lincoln certainly would have been a superb commodity trader. There is a story about Lincoln in his hometown of Springfield, Illinois: he was walking down the street with two boys at his sides, both of whom were making quite a ruckus and crying aloud. A neighbor stopped President Lincoln and asked him what was the matter with the boys. His reply was, "Just what's the matter with the whole world. I've got three walnuts and each wants two."

How emotional of a person are you? If the majority of your business or personal decisions are made on whim and emotion, commodity trading is probably not for you. But if you can be analytical in your decision-making process, I think you are going to find some gargantuan opportunities in the commodity markets over the next few years.

Commodities and the World

If you do become a commodity trader, I'm certain you will find your understanding of the world is enhanced, as you will be exposed on a daily basis to inter-national happenings, whether it's changes in interest rates in London that are affecting the pound and the yen; droughts in Afghanistan that affect the price of cocoa; crop failures in our own country, weather conditions in the sugar-belt of the globe; or high interest rates, which means housing prices are down, so the lumber prices collapse. You will suddenly gain a depth and insight into the economic order of the world that very few people have. That alone makes it worthwhile to trade the commodity market.

You are always thinking in the future, not of where prices are today, but what is going to be happening four or five weeks or three to six months from now. You will be perceiving and playing a game of life on a different level than 99% of all people. You will be playing the game of life in the future, while other people spend most of their lives handling yesterday's problems, you will be handling and dealing with things as they *will be*.

Perhaps the greatest advantage of trading commodities is that commodities have substantial moves, feast or famine. If there is a drought and a shortage of crops, prices move up. By the same token, if there is an over-abundance of crops, prices move down as large supply invariably means lower prices.

In peace-time most countries, including this one, have the ability to increase their agricultural production, which means we have an over-supply, so prices decline. In times of a crisis or war, the nation gears up for national defense, so there is a shortage of agricultural commodities with a concomitant rise in price. Irrespective of what happens, we will see substantial swings in the commodity markets over the next few years. Trading commodities is not only the hottest game in town, it is the most sophisticated game in town. There have been more substantial fortunes made in trading commodities in the last five years by people starting with next to nothing, less than $5,000, than in any other investment vehicle I have studied.

If you delve into this fascinating world, I would like to say to you, "Good luck, and good trading."

4

Take Stock—The Market Also Rises: The Second Best Investment Opportunity of the '80s

Variety in the Market

Next to trading commodities (see Chapter Three), there is no easier and more enjoyable way to make a living or a substantial investment profit than by trading in the Stock Market.

There are no finders fees to pay, no business licenses, very few regulatory agencies to contend with, you need no employees, and, best of all, the cost of entry is substantially lower than in virtually any other form of business.

The best opportunity in the stock market comes from the wide diversification of stocks listed on the country's major exchanges. Growing businesses need capital, and to get it they sell stock in their corporations. They get their capital and we the public get the opportunity to invest in them and ride the waves of fortune and famine they may enjoy. Since there is such great variety you can invest in any sort of company you want: toymakers like Mattel, typewriter manufacturers like IBM, oil drillers like Houston Oil and Gas, gambling equipment manufacturers like Bally, and even casino operators, like Harrah's.

If these don't quite suit your taste, there are always entertainment stocks like RCA, fast food companies like MacDonald's, liquor companies like Hublein, and so on. If you think there is going to be a substantial change, economically speaking, in milling companies, shoemakers, tool-and-dyemakers, auto manufacturers, solar equipment, fishing supplies, or electronic equipment, you will find stocks in these very fields. These stocks will come in many colors and shades, and some will be better than others.

The Great Stock Game

While this variety is certainly the stock exchange's greatest draw, it may also be its greatest drawback for the uninformed investor.

Chart 11
Long-Term Stock Market Perspective

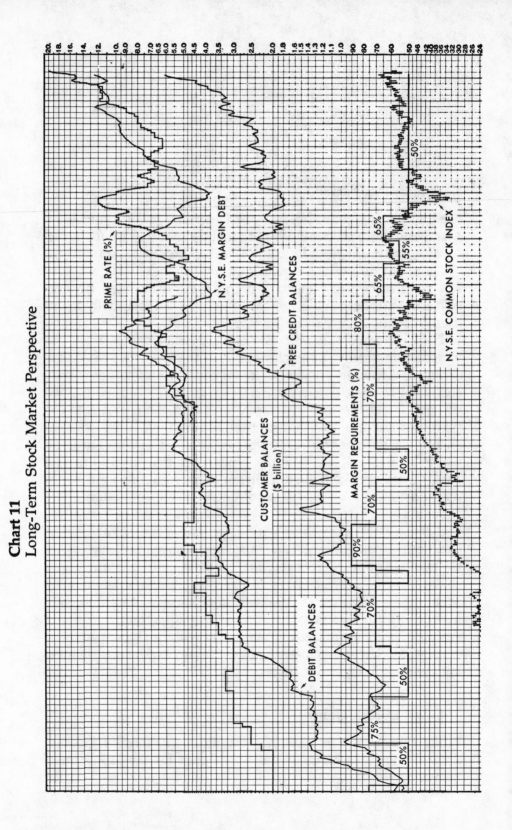

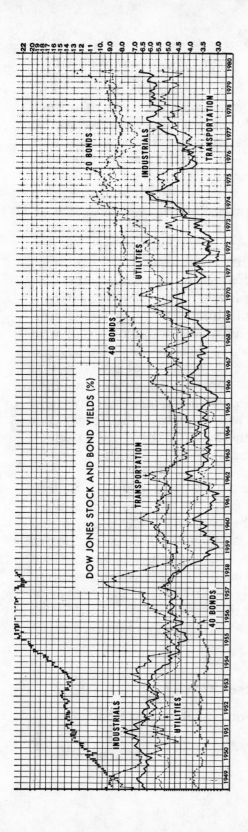

DOW JONES STOCK AND BOND YIELDS (%)

That's because the average investor has a series of difficult decisions to make when he is faced with the more than three thousand listed securities that trade on an active basis in this country. His problem becomes one of first narrowing down and deciding which field he wishes to enter. I hope after reading this book and doing your homework you will have an idea of the types of groups and companies that should perform substantially above-average during the rest of this century.

So, before you rush out and start buying stock, you do need a bit of education, which I hope to give you. Perhaps the first thing you need to know is what can happen in a potentially strong market. For the rest of the decade I envision something similar to what took place in the '60s (see Chart 11), which enjoyed a very substantial, bullish market. What we've been going through since 1966 has been a sideways market with wild upward and downward gyrations. We have already discussed why the stock market hasn't really gone anyplace. Now that politics and economics are in controlled and well-qualified hands, I expect to see the type of sustained upward movement we saw in the '60s. Sure, there will be drops along the way. But the overall trend should be one of a rising market in which huge fortunes will be made. And some of those fortunes will be made literally overnight.

From 1981 to 1983, you're going to see and hear an avalanche of bearish, downcast reports from the doom-and-gloomers, who are now forecasting that the world is literally going to Hell economically, socially, and morally. They will do everything to shake everyone out of present stockholdings and to convince them to stay away entirely from the market. Under scrutiny these bearish arguments simply don't hold up. The demise of the U.S. stock market, just like the demise of the United States itself, has been oversold; it has been so widely advertised that it will never occur.

How to Time Your Stock-Market Activity

There are really only two questions that you ever have to answer when you trade in the stock market. The first is: is this the right time to purchase, or is there some economic factor affecting the entire stock market and/or that particular group of stock that should make me hold back? The second is: is the company I wish to invest in financially sound, with prospects of making more money, and growing still more?

There are a good many books that talk about stock selection. I'm going to do a little bit of that. But before you buy a stock, I feel that it is even more critical for you to select that stock at the right time.

I first began trading in the stock market in 1966. I had the good fortune in that year to buy stock just as the market experienced a profound upswing, in October. As you can see from the charts shown earlier, that was at the tail end of the 1966 bear market and just at the beginning of a gargantuan two-and-a-half year upward spiral.

I was dumb lucky in being at the right place at the right time, and profited immensely. At that time not much attention was focused on market timing. Most approaches to the market were concerned with the fundamental value of stock—was a particular stock over- or under-valued, and, on that basis, was it worthy of purchase. That was 1966 thinking.

Then, in the late '60s and early '70s a group of us dedicated virtually all our research to *timing* as a factor not only of market averages but of individual stocks as well. The results of that research have brought us immeasurably further in our ability to predict major stock highs and lows.

I believe, based on this research, that you can buy almost any stock at a major market low and show substantial profit later on. By the same token, you can sell stock and/or sell short at a major stock market high, and again you are going to reap substantial profit.

Now, if you like you can do what I did and spend five to ten years of pure stock-market analysis, running simulations on computers, researching indicators, and developing your own indicators which help to show those stocks that are to alter substantially in value.

What Sort of Advice You Should Take

Or you can take a short cut and subscribe to the advisory services that have a superb track-record of predicting stock-market alterations. The recommendations I am about to give you I do not give lightly. These are people that, for the most part, I know personally and have had dealings with for a long time. I have followed their work just as they have followed mine, and I have nothing but the utmost respect for them as brilliant market technicians and predictors.

Martin Zweig
747 Third Avenue
New York, N.Y. 10017

Garside Forecast
P.O. Box 1812
Santa Ana, Calif. 92702

Ned Davis
P.O. Box 2089
Venice, Fla. 33595

Gil Haller
State Line, Nevada 89449

Stockmarket Logic
3471 North Federal Highway
Fort Lauderdale, FL 33306

Professional Timing
P.O. Box 7843
Missoula, Montana 59807

Consensus of Insiders
Perry Wysong
Box 1018
Ft. Lauderdale, FL 33305

It should be noted that I run Professional Timing out of the beautiful "Big Sky" country of Montana. You might think that that is a strange and unusual place for a stock-market advisory service, but thanks to the superb communications throughout the world today, it's possible to trade the market from just about anyplace on the globe. I would like to use Professional Timing as an example of just how important timing is in the market place. Don't think I am saying that my advisory service is better than the others I have listed. We all, I think, do a pretty good job. But the figures from Professional Timing should drive home to you the importance of doing the right thing at the right time in the stock market.

The Chase Supply/Demand
Formula Approach

The Professional Timing Advisory Service uses the "formula approach" for trading on the stock market. This means, quite simply, that a method has been devised to tell us when to get in and out. The one we use is the Supply/Demand Formula as developed by Henry Wheeler Chase in the 1940s. I purchased the formula and we have made some changes and improvements in it over the years. Suffice it to say that the signals we use for our published report are real, up-to-the-minute signals given by the stock market. They are not hindsight signals, showing us what we should have done had we known what we know today. That latter is not a bad approach to the stock market, but it is not as significant as current experience and knowledge.

Here is how it works. On April 17, 1962, the Dow Jones Industrial Average stood at 685 and, on that day, the Supply/Demand Formula issued a "sell" signal. It was time, the Formula was saying, to liquidate stock and even, if one were so inclined, to sell short. As of now, as this chapter is being written, the Dow Jones stands at 950, showing a net gain of 335 points over nineteen years.

Now, since that April 17th, nineteen years ago, the Supply/Demand Formula has issued 71 different signals. Of these 71 signals, 59 of them have proved correct, meaning that the formula has been accurate 83% of the time! But what comes next is even more astonishing: while the Dow Jones Industrial Average's net change was only 335 points during almost two decades, the net gain of Dow Points by buying and selling according to the Supply/Demand Formula signals was 3,559 points. 3,559 points!

As the Bible says, "There is a time to sow, and a time to reap." In the stock market, timing your sowing and reaping is what separates the men from the boys and the inexperienced from their money.

My advice to you, then, is either to develop your own stock forecasting tools and formulae, or to rely on the people who are the best in the business at the stock-timing game. These men and I do not always agree; that's natural. But none of us is a perpetual bear or bull. We are all realists who attempt to leave our emotions and biases behind us, so that we can forecast what the market will do with the highest possible degree of accuracy.

How to Attune Yourself to the Future to Make Money Today

The other question you have to resolve is: what particular stocks should I trade? The simplest technique, and, unfortunately, the most difficult to develop, is to attune yourself to the future. If you had the vision to understand the significance of the changes Xerox was bringing to reproduction, you would have made yourself untold fortunes simply by buying Xerox stock and holding on.

But don't think, as the popular press would have you think, that you just have to focus on the electronic marvels of the future. Rather, take the case of "Toys R Us," the supermarket retailer of children's toys. It has proved to be a big, big winner in the stock market. It began trading in 1978 at less than fifty cents a share. Sales skyrocketed, and by January 1980 the company earnings were estimated at $460 million, with a net earning per share of $2.50. The stock that you could have bought for less than half a dollar three years ago is now trading in the $20–$30 range, representing a phenomenal gain of almost 8,000%.

An even more spectacular stock has been Resorts International. It was originally a dull little issue called the Mary Carter Paint Company, but recently it moved away from the paint business and into the resort business, purchasing resorts in the Bahamas, Marine World, and Marine Park. It also entered the gambling business in Nassau and has most recently been a prime mover in resort and casino construction in Atlantic City, N.J., the East Coast's answer to Las Vegas. In 1974, you could have purchased Resorts International Class "A" common stock at about $1.00 per share. Now it sells for $20.00 a share. In just seven years.

But by far the most remarkable case of all has been Houston Oil and Gas. In 1971 it sold for $2.00 to $3.00 a share; in 1973 came the incredible gas shortages; by 1981 the stock was selling for *$88.00* a share. Let's say you had been astute enough to buy 1,000 shares at $2.50 a share in 1971, making a grand total of $2,500.00. In just nine sweet years your investment of $2,500.00 would have been worth $1½ million. All of that tax-free, of course, since you would still be holding onto the original stock. Since you have not sold it, you have no capital gains to report. You could, however, borrow against your $1½ million as a way of cashing in on your chips without suffering taxation. More important, however, is that the stock is currently paying a dividend of 80 cents per share. With your 29,992 shares (taking stock splits into account) you would currently be receiving $23,993 a year in dividends. In other words, you would be receiving, yearly, almost ten times the amount of your original investment, while holding onto capital that has increased about 900 times in value.

Now, this is not particularly unique—a good situation, yes indeed, one of the best, but *not necessarily unique*. It is just indicative of the tremendous profit opportunities that came up in the last few years, which the doom-and-gloomers would have us believe were uniformly "bad times."

How to Choose the Right Low-Priced Stock: The Three-Year Criterion

The similarity between "Toys R Us," Resorts International and Houston Oil is not that they produce any sort of similar product, but rather that in each case company earnings showed substantial improvement. Perhaps the easiest way of making certain that you have a good stock in mind is to find out whether the earnings reported by the company have been up for at least the past three years. If your company has had three consecutive years of higher earnings, it's a pretty good bet.

The problem is that there are literally thousands of low-priced stocks listed on the various exchanges and you've got to be very careful that the stocks you like do meet the three-year criterion. Using that alone, you can weed out about 95% of the stocks around.

The Virtue of the Low-Priced Stock, and the Margin of Profit Rule

An exponential law of mathematics may help you to decide on

low-priced stock rather than on higher-priced stock. Simply put, it is much easier for a stock to go from $2.00 to $20.00 than for a stock to go from $20.00 to $200.00. Lower-priced stocks are the ones most likely to have the most meaningful, substantial, and profitable upswings.

I also suggest you apply to the stock you wish to buy what I call the "Margin of Profit Rule." Subtract the total costs and expenses of the corporation from its net sales: the resulting figure is known as that corporation's "operating income." Next, divide the net sales into the operating income, and you will have what is known as the "Margin of Profit": the profit the company is making on each dollar it spends. This is perhaps the single most important method of telling whether the company you are looking at has what it takes to climb dramatically in price. If there is one sure thing we can say about the stock market, it is that stock prices tend to rise almost hysterically with earnings increases and to decline equally hysterically when earnings fall. Therefore, you need to know whether a company is increasing or decreasing its earnings.

The Art of Bargain-Hunting in the Stock Market

Of the various approaches to trading or investing in the stock market, I would have to give my nod of approval to the purchase of concept stocks that have enjoyed hefty increases in earnings. Now, for the most part I am thinking of stocks that are upwardly mobile or are, at the time you wish to purchase, in an advancing trend. They are bargains not only because they are low-priced today relative to the past, but because they are low-priced relative to their own potential. That's why Tandy-Radio Shack was such a superb buy several years ago. The stock was not necessarily cheap, as compared with what it had been, but given predictable innovations in home-computer technology as well as the increasing demand of the American public for that technology, the price of the stock has appreciated rapidly.

So that's one form of bargain-hunting: finding something that's a bargain relative to tomorrow's prices. However, the more common method of bargain-hunting is to buy something today because its price is low relative to what it has been over the last few years.

I have studied two approaches which seem to do a pretty good job of aiding one in the purchase of low-priced stocks before they enjoy substantial upswings.

Three-Year Market Fluctuation

One of the simplest ways of finding a good, low-priced stock which should go through an immediate surge in price is to observe its market fluctuation over the last three years.

All you have to do is check out what the lowest price of the stock has been in each of the last three years. Next, check which of the prices is the lowest. This price should be your "bargain-basement"; you *should not buy* when the stock is lower than this price. Next, to make certain you are not buying the stock before it dips even more seriously, you should make sure that the stock has *not* dipped lower each consecutive year. Let's say a stock goes from a low point one year of 23, to a low point of 22 the following year, and finally to a low of 21 in the third year. This would not make a good buy candidate, because it has had progressively lower lows each year. What you are looking for is a stock whose lows have held themselves up in some general trading range. Let's take a stock whose low one year is 50; the following year 56; the third year 52. Then, if in the year you are planning to buy the stock it has declined again into the 50 range, you have a superb candidate. However, you should not buy it if it dips lower than 50; 50 is your basement figure.

This is a very good method, but I would prefer you do not use it exclusively. I would prefer that you use it to screen out potentially bad investments, and narrow down your list of potentially rewarding candidates for investment. Now you're not going, in the end, to have very many of these rewarding candidates, but when you do you should next investigate the various companies and their balance sheets to see what the future portends. If it looks as though a company is profitable, has a large hold on its own market, and is run by an aggressive management committed to increased future earnings, you may well, at last, have a superb opportunity to buy.

The Base Price and Sideways Holding Pattern

There's another attractive technique for purchasing bargain basement stocks that incorporates not only price action but also the fundamentals of the specific company as well. For chartists, this is a simple matter: just review a chart, and see whether there is a low point, at least three years ago, that has not yet been violated on the down side. If this is the case, you will see that the stock has been in a "basing pattern," moving back and forth for a period of at least three years.

Then—this is the complicated part—take the lowest price seen in the last three years, and multiply it by 1.618. This constant is a harmonic of the Fibonacci Numerical System that has, for complex reasons, relevance to stock trading. When and if prices rally and close near this last number (the lowest price x 1.618) you can usually rest assured that prices are indeed going up.

The Seasonal Influence

Business trends are seasonal. For example, automobiles sell best in the third quarter of the year, while toys sell best during those three weeks preceding Christmas. This seasonal influence has an impact on stock prices: the following seasonal trading map, courtesy of the *1981 Stock Traders' Almanac*, gives you a good idea of how some of the major stock-market groups are impacted on a seasonal basis (note in particular the automobile and television stock lines). These are based more on consumer patterns than on anything else; but consumer-buying patterns also have seasonal biases to them.

Merrill Lynch discovered, in a study of the 1954-1964 period, that seven major industries—including air-conditioning, meat-packing, aerospace, agricultural machinery and railroads—would have made better trading investments than buy-and-hold investments (Chart 13). If one had just simply bought and held stock in, say, an air-conditioning company, and had held that stock, the ten-year gain would have been 70%, whereas if one had bought and sold based on the *seasonal*

Chart 12
Seasonal Tendency of Stock Market Prices

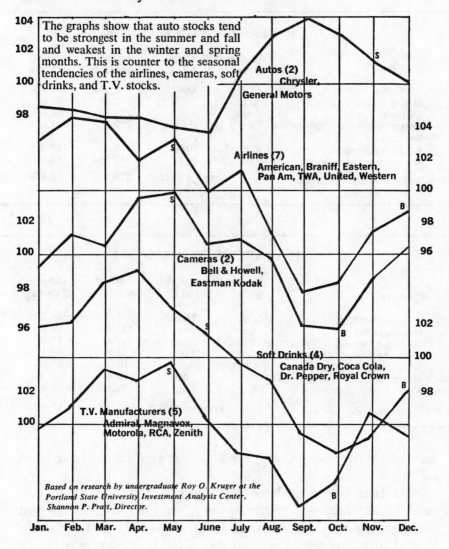

The graphs show that auto stocks tend to be strongest in the summer and fall and weakest in the winter and spring months. This is counter to the seasonal tendencies of the airlines, cameras, soft drinks, and T.V. stocks.

Autos (2)
Chrysler, General Motors

Airlines (7)
American, Braniff, Eastern, Pan Am, TWA, United, Western

Cameras (2)
Bell & Howell, Eastman Kodak

Soft Drinks (4)
Canada Dry, Coca Cola, Dr. Pepper, Royal Crown

T.V. Manufacturers (5)
Admiral, Magnavox, Motorola, RCA, Zenith

Based on research by undergraduate Roy O. Kruger at the Portland State University Investment Analysis Center, Shannon P. Pratt, Director.

Jan. Feb. Mar. Apr. May June July Aug. Sept. Oct. Nov. Dec.

Chart 13
Seasonal Trading Table; 10-Year Results

10-YEAR PROFITS 1954-1964

Industry	Seasonal Strategy BUY	SELL	Trading Seasonally	Holding 10 Years
Air Conditioning	Oct.	March	347.2%	63.4%
Meatpacking	Sept.	Feb.	313.8	81.9
Machine Tools	Sept.	April	235.8	82.5
Property/Liability Insurance	Oct.	Feb.	222.5	104.6
Aerospace	Sept.	Jan.	215.7	36.8
Eastern Railroads	Oct.	Feb.	165.4	49.3
Agricultural Machinery	Oct.	Feb.	145.0	72.5
*Excluding all commissions and taxes		Average Profit*	235.0%	70.1%

10-YEAR PROFITS 1965-1975

Industry	Seasonal Strategy BUY	SELL	Trading Seasonally	Holding 10 Years
Air Conditioning	Oct.	March	48.1%	—27.3%
Meatpacking	Sept.	Feb.	149.6	16.0
Machine Tools	Sept.	April	117.0	—41.6
Property/Liability Insurance	Oct.	Feb.	56.4	45.1
Aerospace	Sept.	Jan.	62.6	—51.8
Railroads (replaces East R.R.)	Oct.	Feb.	64.0	—22.0
Agricultural Machinery	Oct.	Feb.	78.6	— 1.4
*Excluding all commissions and taxes		Average Profit*	82.3%	—11.9%

tendencies of these groups, the ten-year gain would have been 235%.

Yale Hirsch has updated the Merrill Lynch findings with another ten-year survey, this time from 1965 to 1975. As you can see in Chart 13, seasonal influences still are sufficiently strong to make seasonal market-trading a far better strategy than buying and holding. Seasonal trading was not as spectacularly profitable in the '65–'75 period, simply because the market was not that spectacular. Nonetheless, the average profit from trading on a seasonal basis during those ten years was 82%, whereas holding onto a seasonal stock netted people a loss of almost 12%.

The lesson is clear: if you are going to invest seriously in the stock market, you should pay attention to the seasonal influences on the stock you are going to buy. It may well be that careful research and analysis will show you there is indeed a time to buy and a time to sell your particular stock.

More on Playing the Players

In the chapter on commodities, I told you that I think the best way of finding out what is going to happen in the commodity market is to see what the "Big Boys" are doing, to follow the people who have a good record of successfully forecasting the markets.

The same thing can be done in the stock market, in a variety of ways. One of the best ways is to find brokerage firms that are bringing new issues public and whose new issues have a record of very good performance. I'd like to call your attention to OTC Net, Inc., 3600 S. Bealer, Denver, Colorado, 80327. They have brought some companies public with rather spectacular results in the last two years. They were the underwriter for Advanced Monitoring Systems, which went from $.50 a share to $8.00 a share; American Telenet, went from $.10 a share to $.22 a share; Aqua-Culture Production Tech, which went from $.10 a share to $.12 a share; Denver Western Petroleum, which went from $.10 a share to $1.19 a share; Excalibur Technologies, which went from $1.00 a share to $3.25 a share; International Remote Imaging Systems, Inc., which went from $1.00 a share to $4.12 a share; Neo-Bionics, Inc., which went from $.50 a share to $1.87 a share; North American Energy Resources, which went from $.10 a share to $.72 a share; and Royalty Development, which came at $1.00 a share, and is currently trading at $1.00 a share.

The average gain on these stocks is 462%; again, all this taking place at a time when the world was supposedly falling apart, and the American economy on its way to a bottomless pit!

White House Stock: Presidential Influence on Market Figures

Regardless of how you feel about the powers that be in the White House, whether now or twenty years from now, there are lessons to be learned about the relation of President to stock market, or, more specifically, of the Presidential term to stock-market activity.

The first thing that past records show is that that the first year in office, no matter who the President is or what he does, will be a down-year on Wall Street. Then, as the President's second year begins, things get a little better; the market advances almost 8% during the President's second year.

Things really get moving, though, in the third, or "economically explosive," year of a President's term. In this year the market rallies stunningly, making an average gain of over 16%. In the fourth and final year of the term, prices still are tending to post gains, but not on the order of the second and third years.

I first wrote about this fascinating correlation in my first stock-market book, published in 1972. This is not a new idea; it has been around for a while. What is interesting to note is that in 1972 I clearly forecast what was to happen in 1977, Carter's first year in office—stock prices dropped from the 1,000 area to the 800 area. In his second year of office, stock prices rallied from the previous year's low of 740 to a 920 high in the autumn. In the third year, stock prices opened around 780, rallying in the summer of the year to 900, yet still closed at 840. Finally, in the fourth year, there were scattered unbalanced gains. So we see that the greatest opportunity in the stock market was to be had in the third year of Carter's term, from the low point of the second year to the high point of the third, and *was predictable in 1972*. On that basis, I say that 1983 will be the stellar year of the Reagan presidency (or its first term, anyway) on the stock exchanges.

Major Stock Market Buy and Sell Signals Given by the Federal Reserve System

Very seldom will anyone ring a bell on an investment opportunity for you, making it a lead-pipe cinch for you to step in, and take action, which will result later on in taking profits. Investing is simply not that easy. However, there is one definite bell ringer on Wall Street, and that is the Federal Reserve System which began controlling the amount of reserve requirements in banks in 1936. As it eases or contracts credit in America, major stock market moves result. The reason for this is obvious. When money is going to be plentiful, people are going to take that money and invest it. By the same token, when money tightens up, there's not much of it around, there will not be money for companies to expand, and that will affect the price of their stocks; which, accordingly, will experience cut-backs in growth rates, which investors do not like.

There have been seven initial cuts since the Federal Reserve System began manipulating the Reserve requirements. If you were to take those as simple buy indications in the stock market, your performance would have been superb.

My good friend, Marty Zweig, detailed the results of the impact of Federal Reserve moves on the stock market in an article in *Barron's* magazine in June, 1980. A summary of Marty's data is shown here.

As you can see, Table 1 shows when there were seven initial Reserve requirement cuts. In the three-, six-, and twelve-month time zones, following these initial cuts, the average gains of the Dow Jones Industrial Average were almost 6%, almost 17%, and almost 25%. If one had simply held stocks, following all of the Reserve requirement cuts, the annual rate of gain would have been 24.7%; while, if one had simply used the buy and hold strategy on the Dow Jones Industrial Average, not using the Reserve requirement cuts as a timing indication, the annualized rate of gain would have been 3.8%.

Table 2 shows 18 previous cuts that we have seen in the discount rate, which is set by the Federal Reserve System; and, again, you can see the impact of Fed policy on the stock market. Following discount rate cuts, the average increase in the Dow Jones Industrial Average, following a three-month time period was 3.1%; a six-month time period, 10.4%; and a twelve-month time period, 13.8%.

The message should be clear. They do ring bells on Wall Street, and the bell ringer is the Federal Reserve System. When they move to ease credit, by lowering the Reserve requirements

Chart 14
The Federal Reserve Effect

Table I
Initial Reserve Requirement Cuts: 1936 to 1980

Date	% Change Dow Industrials			% Change Zweig Unweighted Price Index		
	3 Mo.	6 Mo.	12 Mo.	3 Mo.	6 Mo.	12 Mo.
4/16/38	+14.9	+25.6	+ 7.4	+ 17.7	+ 26.7	+ .6
8/20/42	+ 7.5	+19.6	+28.0	+ 14.2	+ 44.5	+ 74.4
4/30/49	+ 2.9	+ 9.2	+23.0	− .9	+ 9.0	+ 25.1
7/ 9/53	− 1.5	+ 4.1	+25.8	− 6.0	− 3.4	+ 15.3
2/27/58	+ 5.3	+16.4	+37.9	+ 9.7	+ 23.0	+ 51.1
9/ 1/60	− 5.0	+ 5.9	+15.2	− 5.0	+ 12.7	+ 20.8
11/28/74	+19.4	+32.0	+39.1	+ 19.3	+ 33.3	+ 32.9
5/22/80						
$10,000=	$14,953	$27,785	$47,005	$15,567	$35,621	$60,656
Compounded Return:	+ 5.9%	+15.7%	+24.7%	+ 6.5%	+ 19.9%	+ 29.4%
Annualized Return:	+25.8%	+33.9%	+24.7%	+ 28.8%	+ 43.8%	+ 29.4%
All Other Periods:			+0.2%/Yr.			+1.6%/Yr.
Buy-Hold:			+3.8%/Yr.			+5.6%/Yr.

Table II
Initial Discount Rate Cuts: 1914 to 1980

Date	% Change Dow Industrials			% Change Zweig Unweighted Price Index		
	3 Mo.	6 Mo.	12 Mo.	3 Mo.	6 Mo.	12 Mo.
12/12/14	+ 3.6	+29.1	+76.4	+ 3.6	+ 29.1	+ 76.4
5/ 5/21	−13.8	− 7.5	+16.3	− 13.8	− 7.5	+ 16.3
5/ 1/24	+18.0	+23.6	+44.9	+ 18.0	+ 23.6	+ 44.9
4/23/26	+ 8.4	+ 4.9	+16.8	+ 8.4	+ 4.9	+ 16.8
8/ 5/27	+ 2.7	+ 7.7	+18.6	+ 2.0	+ 12.5	+ 23.0
1/ 1/29	− 2.2	+ .4	−32.5	− 5.9	− .6	− 38.8
2/26/32	−39.0	− 9.8	−37.8	− 37.6	+ 38.5	− 17.2
4/ 7/33	+57.6	+66.1	+76.3	+207.3	+144.2	+210.6
8/27/37	−29.5	−25.6	−19.3	− 35.4	− 35.6	− 29.5
10/30/42	+10.5	+18.4	+21.1	+ 18.3	+ 51.9	+ 55.7
2/ 5/54	+ 8.2	+18.4	+39.5	+ 3.6	+ 16.5	+ 44.1
11/15/57	+ 1.4	+ 4.3	+28.7	+ 5.6	+ 12.8	+ 45.7
6/10/60	− 6.3	− 6.7	+ 7.0	− 2.0	− 2.9	+ 22.7
4/ 7/67	+ 1.9	+ 8.9	+ 1.5	+ 7.8	+ 16.4	+ 8.3
8/30/68	+ 9.9	+ 1.0	− 6.6	+ 12.2	+ .2	− 12.6
11/13/70	+17.0	+23.2	+ 7.0	+ 28.5	+ 31.7	+ 10.2
11/19/71	+13.2	+18.6	+24.0	+ 18.5	+ 17.2	+ 13.3
12/ 6/74	+31.8	+45.3	+41.7	+ 32.1	+ 49.0	+ 36.4
5/ 6/80						
$10,000=	$17,217	$59,448	$101,991	$41,910	$196,072	$306,400
Compounded Return:	+ 3.1%	+10.4%	+13.8%	+ 8.3%	+ 18.0%	+ 20.9%
Annualized Return:	+12.8%	+21.9%	+13.8%	+ 37.5%	+ 39.2%	+ 20.9%
All Other Periods:			+.8%/Yr.			+1.0%/Yr.
Buy-Hold:			+4.2%/Yr.			+6.1%/Yr.

or cutting the discount rate, you had better start getting into the stock market; because the probabilities of a substantial up-move have been greatly enhanced.

This is extremely timely, as the 1980s begin. The discount rate is currently at 14%; which, just like the Reserve requirements, have been continually boosted, since the fall of 1980. You should pay close attention to the discount rate and Reserve requirements. There is an excellent probability that they are going to start dropping. My estimate would be some time in September, 1981. If they have not begun dropping by then, they most likely will begin dropping in the first part of 1982; and that is going to set up a superb buying opportunity.

My forecast for when it happens is not as significant as when it does start taking place and that you hear the bells, gather up your cash, and begin buying American stocks; because you'll have the full impact and power of the mighty Federal Reserve System on your side.

What Stocks to Buy for the Future

There are several conceptual groups right now that I think are going to take off and skyrocket towards the moon in the last decade of this century. In the energy development area, investors should be paying close attention to new drilling and recovery techniques for natural gas and oil, and while there is probably still some type of play left in nuclear fission, the big boom will, in my opinion, come in nuclear fusion. You should read every single thing you can on nuclear fusion and then scout out companies that are supplying technology for it, as well as companies which will be producing energy through fusion.

Hemingway said, "The sun also rises," and I believe it's the rising sun that is going to make a lot of money for investors in solar energy. In the solar area you should certainly follow Solar Industries of Colorado, as well as Safeguard Industries and ACRO Energy. Now, there are two known facts about energy supply. First, at some point in time, hydrocarbon supply on this planet will be expended completely. It is probably a long way off in terms of natural gas: we probably have enough natural gas to last another 1,000 years and enough crude oil to last, perhaps, 200 years. It's there; the question is, at what price? Second, we know there is an eternal supply of unlimited energy around from the sun. Try to comprehend, if you can, that those things we call "solar flares" spurt almost 48,000 miles into space. Those huge balls of energy are going to be tapped by someone and it will mean more profits than all the energy corporations have earned to date. It is further estimated that "sun-spots," actually flare-ups on the surface of the sun which are larger than ten Earths combined, will be tapped sometime in the next fifty years, meaning further fortunes for investors.

Energy Spin-Offs

There is a spin-off market of the energy crisis that investors should also consider. Instead of focusing your attention only on energy sources, you should also expose yourself to new ways of using energy. Certainly the advent of the small, high-mileage car in America is an example of this sort of new product for an old market.

It's been estimated that within seven to ten years, we will have in production cars that run only on electricity, which will be able to cruise at about 60 miles-per-hour and go about 300 miles before recharging. Here is where nuclear fusion may come in; if oil goes out and electricity comes in, look for nuclear power to beef up the pockets of its investors.

Making Money While Saving Lives, Part I

A few years ago, fortunes were made on the "Fuzz Buster," a gizmo that you put in your car which picks up the radar signals of highway patrolmen and warns you to slow down, thus helping you to avoid a ticket. Now two companies in America have surpassed it with two new sonar auto units which do more than merely save you from speeding tickets. These units can be placed behind the grill of a car and in the trunk. They emit sonar signals that bounce off objects in front of and behind the car. A mini-computer then tells the driver with beeps and other electronic signals how many cars there are in the road and where they are in relation to him. This will be a wonderful way of preventing accidents. Sonar scopes are bound to make money if they can be marketed at an affordable price, and is a good investment opportunity.

Making Money by Saving Lives, Part II

You should also consider what we could loosely label "health care/life extension" discoveries. You are probably well aware of the profits corporations have made off of heart transplants, pacemakers and heart monitors. What you may not know is that more people suffer from hearing and speech disorders than from most all diseases combined. Now, I've just got to think that some bright and enterprising doctor or research group is going to come up with improvements in the treatment of hearing and speech disorders some time within the next twenty years, and when that happens investors will profit wildly.

Senility is becoming a greater problem as our life expectancy increases. Consider, then, if you will, the research of Dr. Kenneth Davis, who has reported success in memory improvement with the drug Physostigmine. Davis claims that he has restored up to 14% of the memories of various aged people. The drug apparently works by increasing the level of Choline in the brain. Such a drug is worthy of much attention by possible investors.

Physical Improvement Stocks

If you want to get even more wild and venture into the realm of what we normally think of as science-fiction, you should turn your attention to the advances in bionic medicine. We've already seen the use of complete hip-joint replacement; such operations are now numbering more than 80,000 a year. Finger- and knee-joint replacements are now occurring frequently. There has already been work done on intra-ocular lens implants for vision correction, and the bionic arm you have seen on television is now becoming a reality. Experts from the Medical Products Division of General Atomic Company and the Rancho Los Amigos Hospital put together a bionic (or "myo-electric") arm in 1975. People have already been fitted with them, and can tie their shoes and manipulate fingers; obviously this would have been a wild dream for an amputee twenty years ago.

Here is a quick list of some of things that have been done in bionics: artificial skin, implanted corneas, chin implants, artificial lungs, breast augmentation, artificial hearts and heart valves, artificial esophaguses, artificial livers, synthetic tendons, artificial arms, and artificial legs. In fact, there are now available some 150 different types of knee joints, and some 50 different types of artificial ankles, some so sophisticated that they have sensors in the heel to make certain the wearer does not lose his balance.

I don't think we are going to see Steve Austin, the "Six Million Dollar Man," walking around, but we are going to be able to improve the flaws in the human body with bionics. Companies that make these bionic products should see phenomenally rapid appreciation of their stock value.

Making People and Making Money

But perhaps bionics is not quite far out enough for you. For you, there is always genetic engineering, as carried out by such firms as Biogen, S.A.

Almost all bio-genetic firms are directing their attentions to the production of Interferon, the wonder-drug. IF (as it is called) is a natural protein that seems to have a shotgun effect upon viral diseases, including cancer. Some researchers even claim it helps to increase one's life-span. If IF is passed by the FDA and works as well as they say it does, the profits should be unbelievable. Pharmaceuticals companies might well be the best investment for the future.

The most common problem we will see, looking back from the year 1999 to the early 1980s, is that our minds were not expansive or creative enough to envision the opportunities and developments that would take place. I am convinced most of us do not fully understand the developments that high technology is going to bring into existence. Thus, we may think some of the proposals are too far-fetched; when, in fact, they are not far-fetched enough.

A good example would be the case of a little company called Pure Cycle, that has developed a way of totally recycling water for personal consumption. For approximately $15,000, one can purchase one of their units; which, when filled with 500 gallons of water, would provide all of the water that a house needs on a permanent and on-going basis. All of the water is recycled through their unit, with an estimated net loss of approximately four gallons per year. The rest of it, from sewage to showers, dish-water to drinking water, is recycled through a small recycling plant that will probably be as common in some homes as today's freezer or refrigerator.

This is especially true of desert homes, mountain homes, or homes in communities where there is a shortage of water and/or of sewage facilities. In some areas it is not possible to build now, because one cannot get a water permit. However, with a Pure Cycle unit, that would not be a problem. One's total water and sewage is self-contained within the home, and on a totally recyclable basis. Obviously, this is good news for millions of people in many parts of the world. It is even better news for investors who get in at the right time.

The "First-In" Investment Strategy

The truly intelligent investor will try his utmost to buy the stock of the first company that gets into one of these growth areas. One of the truisms of business is that the first in a field stays the longest and makes the most money. Many companies make computers, but IBM was the initial leader in the field and remains its dominant force, in large part due to the public's understanding of IBM's venerability. IBM is number one in their minds because IBM was the first in.

This applies to virtually everything we consume, whether it be computers or Coca-Cola. Coke continues to be the dominant cola beverage not because it tastes any better than the others but simply because Coke was first. And being first has paid off. The same goes with Eastman Kodak and cameras.

The position a company maintains may well be more important than its product and the quality of its product. The best example of this was the head-to-head battle between RCA and IBM over computers. The September 19, 1970, issue of *Business*

Week put it simply: "RCA Fires Broadside at Number One." IBM was "number one," and the story was that RCA was going to get into the multibillion dollar computer business. It looked like a natural. RCA had a good name, was a well-established company; it should have been able to cut into IBM's market. Robert Sarnoff, the Chairman of RCA, said that the company had spent "far more to develop a strong position in the computer industry than we have ever put into any business venture." But two years and $250 million later, RCA pulled out of the computer business lock, stock and barrel.

The message is clear. There is very little chance of success if you invest in a company that seeks to establish itself in a well-occupied and established field. You should look for "first-in" corporations yourself, some of which I have given you an idea of in this chapter.

5

Real Estate— How to Deal in the Third Best Investment Opportunity of the '80s

The Three Best Investments

The greatest investment opportunities in the next twenty years should come from the commodity market, for the individual who has the time, patience, skill and desire to dance among the risks and rewards of this volatile world. I say this because the gains in the commodity market are so spectacular. It is not unusual to make 50% to 60% on your money in one day in the commodity market, if you're on target. Thus, an accurate or perfect commodity trader will always reap rewards twenty to thirty times those to be gotten elsewhere.

Right behind commodities will be the stock market, because of the tremendous technological changes that corporate America will see in the next quarter of a century. The American consumer is going to be spending billions of dollars over the next twenty years, and those dollars will improve the earnings of stocks listed on the exchange. It will quadruple those prices several times over. That's a bold statement; *but it will take place.* You will see stocks rising from four to fifteen times their current market value by the end of the decade.

The third best investment, and in one respect, the best investment for the average person, is real estate. Real estate prices will also increase over the next twenty years, although not as dramatically as some stocks will. The advantage is that real estate is an easier game to play. One needs less information and has more control. One of the problems with stocks or commodities is that you have absolutely no control over what will happen, whether a war breaks out in Israel, or there's crop failure or blight; there are many factors that always blindside the commodity or stock investory. That, of course, can happen to some extent in real estate, but usually, most of the factors are known and are under the investor's control. Thus, my suggestion for the average person who has some money but not the time to devote to the study and understanding of the various marketplaces, is to focus his attention on real estate.

Getting a License

The very best real estate investment you will ever make, even if you do not become a serious real estate investor, would be to get your real estate license. Let me explain why I am so adamant that you get your real estate license. The average family owns at least four different homes in a lifetime. That means a total of eight real estate transactions, because with each new home you are selling one and buying another. If each home has an average price of $75,000, you will be buying and selling $600,000 of real estate. Figuring a standard brokerage commission of 6% on just the home sales alone, the non-licensed home-owner will incur commission charges of approximately $36.000. Not all, but some of those fees can be recovered if you have a real estate broker's license. If you're not in real estate— I'm not heavily involved in it myself—you probably have an aversion to getting your real estate license and hanging around with some of the real estate crowd. Some of them are even worse than commodity traders or advisors! Nonetheless, the economics of the situation simply makes it mandatory that you secure a real estate license. Your total investment for the license will almost certainly be less than $1,000; you will save tens of thousands of dollars. Of course, if you plan on doing any other buying and selling in the real estate markets, you will have additional commission charge savings on top of that $36,000.

Everybody Wants Land

The second best real estate advice I can give you is advice you've probably already heard, but with a new twist. The advice was originally given, I believe, by Will Rogers, who told people: "Buy land because they aren't making any more of it." That is good and true, but it doesn't tell today's investors specifically what land to purchase.

My own personal real estate experience and study of the real estate market indicate that regardless of where you live, whether in downtown New York City, Diamond Head, Hawaii, La Jolla, California, or Palm Beach, Florida, there is one basic real estate rule that will make you more money than all the real estate text books combined will ever teach you.

There's a law in economics that "good money will drive out

bad." In real estate, this can be translated to: "Good money will also drive up the value of good properties". This means that the properties most likely to appreciate rapidly over the next coming few years will be the properties that have already been bid to premiums, and are considered "outrageously expensive." There will be some exceptions to this rule, based on demographic trend changes, but by and large, the one rule that will make you the most money trading real estate is to buy the property that's been selling for the most money. This is particularly true if you buy property that does not produce income, but is used for residential or recreational purposes.

Property that is already selling at higher prices than property around it didn't get so expensive by chance. It got expensive because investors and purchasers felt that *that* piece of land had more value. That's why they were willing to part with more of their hard-earned cash: they thought they were getting more. Perhaps the size of the lot was smaller, but all factors considered they were willing to give more money for a small piece of land because there was something intrinsic there that made that property more valuable.

The best example of this is oceanfront property. Will Rogers once said, "They just aren't making any more [coast-line]," and coast-line property has been bid to a premium. It is going to continue being bid to premium after premium after premium, as it becomes more and more difficult to get new coast-line property. Those who have coast-line property currently have something that is in very small supply with very large demand. Basic economics tells us that such property will go up in value more rapidly than other property throughout the country.

The Attractions of Property

So, whether you live in Tallahassee, Chicago, Kansas City, Oklahoma City, Billings, Montana, or Provo, Utah, I think you'll make the most money the quickest by finding the properties that have sold for the most money and concentrating your efforts on finding property that either duplicates it, but has not been bid up, or simply purchasing it because you know you're going to be able to sell it later on at a profit to someone else. It is the attractiveness of property that makes it worth more.

Property is attractive for one of two reasons: first, intrinsically, as coast-line and mountain properties are; and second, because of changes in and around the property, such as a freeway, shopping centers, man-made lakes, etc.

In the second instance, the rule of "buying high because it's going higher" may not prove as profitable as in the first instance. The first will be your best investment buy in the real estate market. Even if the economy crashes, as the prophets of doom predict, or whether it goes straight up, there will always be enough cash around for people to buy inherently attractive properties.

One of the few things Howard Ruff and I agree upon is the type of real estate that will be profitable and make a good investment over the coming years. Ruff and his crowd foresee a steady price movement in rural America. It is a fact that people from the large cities will begin migrating to rural areas. It just so happens that I am one of those people. I live in one of the most ideal places in America, a pollution-free, snow-capped mountain valley, with one of the largest fresh-water lakes in the Rocky Mountains stretching out almost 28 miles below us. We are less than an hour drive to one of America's most spectacular and beautiful parks, Glacier National Park; less than 20 minutes drive from skiing at Big Mountain Ski Resort; adjacent to the lake for boating, water-skiing, and fishing for lake trout that run up to 30 pounds. In addition to that, we have very good electronic communications, as well as excellent airline connections.

Don't get me wrong. I'm not working for the Chamber of Commerce. I just want you to know that I have some experience living in the type of area that Ruff and others have discussed.

Before living in Kalispell, Montana, I lived in Carmel, California, an equally gorgeous area on the coast of the Pacific. There are many similarities between Carmel and Kalispell, and both places exemplify the sort of real-estate opportunity that depression forecasters would have you buy.

However, property values have not particularly soared in the Flathead Valley where I live now. They have in California, in Carmel; and I think the reason is that Carmel is closer to the

urban areas than Kalispell. We're simply a long way from anywhere, which is the way many of us like it; but because of that,
we do not have the commercial enterprise and activity that a
Carmel, La Jolla or Palm Beach has.

Sure, people do migrate to Montana, looking for a small
town to live in, but those tend to be pretty stable people, not
the high rollers with tons of money sticking out their hip pockets. They're people who want to get their families out of the
drug scene in Chicago or Dallas, and are willing to give up a
good paying job there for a less than average paying salary in
Montana. There are not the type of people that have enough
money to alter real-estate prices radically, at least not in a short
period of time. Nonetheless, the demand factor dictates that
the price of land in areas like Kallispell will continue to
increase.

The Effect of the Fed on Real Estate

Another rule of the real estate game is that there will be direct
changes in real-estate prices and values, depending on the
credit expansion and contraction of the Federal Reserve System. We have now almost 40 years of data that presents a
rather convincing case: the Federal Reserve System increases
our borrowing power by expanding the rate at which banks can
loan or by lowering interest. Then more money goes into circulation and that money drives up real estate prices higher. Thus,
the ideal time for a cash buyer is during a time of economic
recession, when there has been a down-turn in the money
supply and the faucets on the credit pipes have been turned
off. But as credit is expanding, prices will go up; and the person
with cash—a hard-earned, tangible asset—will have to compete with people who are getting easy money from the Fed.
Thus, cash buyers will lose the advantage that cold cash had
during the credit crunch.

How to Cash in on the Highways

One of the old real estate games, and one of the best ones that ever came down the pike, was to buy land near soon-to-be-built turnpikes or freeways and especially at the intersection of two freeways. "X", in fact, did mark the spot of where you should make an investment; build a motel, gas station, restaurant, or what-have-you, for the travelers. But that game has been altered radically in two respects. First, the game has been played; most of the major intersections in the country have been built; and secondly, as I read what's coming out of Washington D.C., we're going to see less emphasis on our national highway program, which means fewer freeways for the future. This market is one that is pretty much locked in, and if someone is promising or suggesting to you that a piece of property is going to have freeways built over it in the future, I would be somewhat skeptical and do my own research most thoroughly. However, if you are in a truly isolated area and a freeway *is* going to come into your real-estate zone, I would not be in the least bit surprised to see real-estate values increase 200% to 400%, as your area opens up to the rest of the country.

There are still ways, however, to play the real-estate highway investment game. One would be to find a strip of land between two cities that are relatively close together. Ideally, the cities should be no more than twenty miles apart, and some growth should be connecting the cities economically. *Buy land right now.* The cheapest land in that situation would be right in the middle, equidistant from the cities. Buy that, because within twenty years it will be developed land, part of the urban sprawl between the two towns. West-coasters may want to take a look at what happened in the Springfield–Eugene, Oregon, area. Those in the Rocky Mountain area should notice what's happened between Provo and Orem, Utah, and almost all the way up to Salt Lake City. Mid-Westerners, of course, have already seen it take place on the grand scale of Minneapolis/St. Paul; while on the East coast we've seen the sprawl take over almost the entire Eastern seaboard. You should check to make certain that the opportunity for growth is equal in both directions, that there are not major bodies of water, mountains, etc., between them. Don't let little things like garbage dumps scare you off, because that's land that can be changed.

How to Make Money at Home

The other way of playing the real estate "road to riches" game, and it's one you can play right where you live, is to thoroughly scout out your home town. Take long, extended and thorough drives on all of the roads that lead out of the center of the town itself. One road may go north, another east, another southwest. Don't worry about that; study each area. The purpose of your study will be to choose the best possible direction in which the city should grow the most quickly. Which of the exits from the town provides the most opportunity for homeowners? In rating opportunity, you should be looking at things such as view, ease of travel, which directions the school systems have begun building up in, major shopping center developments, etc. Once you've figured out what appears to be the direction for the city to grow in, it's simply a question of going out to where real estate values are still low; values will be low, because most people do not have the insight that you will suddenly have acquired. Buy land, sit on it, and wait until the city comes to meet you, because meet you it will. We are a growth economy. In the past some of our growth has been environmentally damaging and founded on whims, instead of intelligent planning; but that day, thank goodness, is just about behind us. The growth will continue; it will just be more orderly. Since you've already done your homework, you know in which direction the order should follow.

In playing the real estate "road" game, the novice investor is usually frightened away from properties, especially housing properties, immediately adjacent to a freeway. Believe it or not, however, you will find a greater and more rapid rise in property value the closer a property is situated to a freeway or major road. Increases in value will be smaller and will occur less often the farther away the property is from the major transportation artery in a developed area.

Real-Estate Scheming

Let's say you've located two cities that will be converging, and you have acquired attractive property at a low price somewhere between the two of them. Believe it or not, you can change history, and make the convergence occur even more quickly, if you are able to locate, say, a very attractive restaurant or office complex, somewhere in or around your property. It does not necessarily even have to be on your property, but if, in your scheming, you can help draw traffic and growth in the direction you want it to go by supporting other projects along the way, you will see the growth that you are expecting move a little more quickly. You should be on guard and aware that other real-estate people are not sitting at home thinking, they're scheming too. The law of self-interest prevails.

Williams' Personal History of Real-Estate Dealing

My own real-estate investment experiences have been enjoyable, certainly not as spectacular as my forages into the stock and commodity markets, but nonetheless, they have been good. For a period of time I owned an office building in Redding, California, which was really an ideal investment situation. The previous owner was a well-established gentleman in town who had over-extended himself during a credit crunch. I was fortunate in that I had cash and was able to buy the building at an extremely low price; you can call it scheming if you like, but it certainly wasn't taking advantage of the individual. He needed my money and I was willing to part with it for the office building at the good price.

As things worked out later, I was in a short cash position, and sold the building to a very good friend of mine; again, at a good price to my friend, certainly not as good a price as I could have gotten; but I did get the cash, which, at that particular point in my life, was more important than an office building.

I've also been involved in owning a motel, although we made most of our money not by renting rooms, but by selling the motel a little bit later on to someone who was more experienced in the motel business. In the motel play, we found an attractive tourist town in southern California that had a shortage of motels. The motel was built through raising funds through a limited partnership and bank loans. We were fortunate to have good management, because in addition to starting the motel, and despite the fact that we were one of the few ones in town, the gas shortage of the '70s began shortly after we opened.

Instead of complaining about the gas shortage, our management schemed and came up with the idea of going after the tour business; after all, tours are on buses, which means only one engine hauling fifty or sixty people. We had great success. The motel was booked almost constantly, and we were able to sell the motel later on for a substantial amount of money.

Another real estate transaction I've been involved in concerns the beautiful town of Sausalito, California. Sausalito has only one hotel or motel in its vicinity. Our thought was to buy a piece of land and build a motel convention center on the site.

The problem with that particular investment was the City Council of Sausalito has taken forever and a day to get final approval for our project's plans. However, again, we schemed, and have continued working with the City Council. Meanwhile, the property value has soared, because we have done the legwork in getting the idea through the City Council. Now, the property has been purchased by a more financially substantial party, who will continue the development work that we began. They were excited and interested in paying us a very fair price for the property, not just because of its intrinsic beauty, and the real dynamite situation of having one of only two motels in one of the largest tourist attraction towns in California, but because we had done the groundwork. Our investment consisted of not only the land, but also the time: time with architects, time with planning commissions, time with the City Council, time getting the people of Sausalito to understand that we were involved in a truly beautiful and environmentally sound project.

Interesting Real-Estate Deals

One of the real-estate investment projects I'm involved in right now is extremely unusual. About four years ago, one of my good friends saw a notice in the *Wall Street Journal* about a town in Michigan, a former military base which the military had left behind. My friend got together a group of partners and we purchased the entire town! That included a golf course, homes, recreational centers; you name it, we've got it. This is a very big undertaking, and my only position was as an investor. My friends who put it together were very astute. They had the best of both worlds, a property that had been taken good care of in an attractive part of the state, being offered at a substantially reduced price for an extraordinary reason: the government moved out.

Since then, the property has been converted for civilian use, and has become a most successful real estate project. The main lesson I learned from this investment is not to let the size of real estate investment programs scare you away. In the stock and commodity markets I'm scared to death of huge positions, because a small move can totally wipe you out. But in the real estate market, you can finance these huge deals through banks and savings and loans, as well as by raising money through limited partnerships. The purchase of the complete city should continue to be a success, not only because it was bought right, but because it fits many of the criteria of the perfect rural community; an attractive area, close yet still removed from the major metropolitan centers of the state.

Buy Scarce

The thing you've got to keep looking for in real estate investments is property that's simply not going to be available in the future. In 1973, I purchase a lake-front property for about $10,000. That property is now worth well over $50,000, because of the scarcity of private lake-front property in the state of Montana. This is the type of property that will appreciate the most rapidly. A lake-front property on a public lake will also appreciate, but since it is not as scarce, or rare, as lake-front property on a private lake, the public lake real-estate investment will not appreciate as rapidly.

I'm not bragging. That was an investment that was really based more on luck, because at that point in my life I had not yet fully formulated how to play the real estate market; but purchasing that property and seeing it accelerate in value much more quickly than other property taught me a lesson I can now share with you.

Money Collectives

I believe that over the next twenty years money pools will occupy important positions in real-estate investment. We've already seen them, of course, in the stock markets and mutual funds; and they have begun operating in the commodity market, with commodity funds. Recently the collective fund has started to come into vogue in the real-estate market, through limited partnership offerings. Limited partnerships can provide tremendous opportunities for the investor. Most of us simply don't have the millions of dollars necessary to put together a good, well-planned major development. And certainly these major developments are the way of the future. So, a group of us can get together, pool our assets, and search out good management, and offer, at the lowest price, the type of real-estate developments that are needed. Thus, I would certainly encourage you to investigate all aspects of limited real-estate partnerships. You should concentrate on management, because, by and large, good management always has good properties. You can have good property and bad management and end up in problems, but I have seen good management with just so-so properties come out ahead.

Farm Land

One of the trends that we may see with limited partnerships is farm land investment. So far, there is still a good opportunity for you to purchase farm land; but as the price of farm land escalates and the size of land needed to have a profitable farm increases, we'll probably see more partnership operations on farm land. Nevertheless, I do want to give you some of my insights on what you should be looking for. First of all, you should know that farm land is probably one of the three or four best real-estate plays over the coming twenty years, for two reasons: first, the farm land is productive; second, farm land, especially farm land close to those rural cities to which Howard Ruff wants you to move, is the land these rural cities will expand upon.

Here you have the best of both worlds. Your farm produces income, while you wait for the city to grow out to you. If you can find this type of farm land, buy it. It's a steal. You can't lose money on it—unless you blow it as a farmer. You should farm the land with all intentions of ultimately selling it for development, in the event that food prices do not rise high enough to make the land profitable. And the intelligent farmer of the 80's and 90's is not going to whack down all of the trees on his property. He's going to keep trees and gullies and natural water sheds, so that later on the property can be developed on a quicker and lower cost basis.

Real Estate is Productive

One of the advantages of farm land is that, regardless of what happens to the economy, farm land values hold up better than raw land values, simply because farm land is productive. If you make some improvements and agriculture prices do edge upwards a little bit, you have a much greater possibility for a long-term gain, even if your yearly production is not terribly profitable.

If you're going to own farm land, you should realize that we've had a switch in agriculture in this country. It used to be that our farms and ranches were labor-intensive, but now they are capital-intensive. Dollars have been substituted for manpower. It used to take five to ten people to run a pretty nice sized ranch; now it can be done with one or two people and a lot of machines. Whether those machines are automatic milkers, or Hondas to round up the cattle, the machine age has had more of an effect on ranching than on just about any other industry besides computers.

Rental Property Is Pretty Good

I am convinced that rental property can present an extremely good opportunity for those with very limited funds. Most everyone knows the game. You move into an old dilapidated house in a nice neighborhood, fix it up, sell it, and move on to another dilapidated house in another neighborhood, fix that house up and sell it. After two or three sales, you're going to have realized a nice profit for your work; and then perhaps you can buy a larger house, fix it up and sell it for even more money. This becomes almost a pyramid scheme, moving from one house to another. There is a problem with it, though, for many people. Some people, like myself, are about as adept with hammers and paint brushes as the "Incredible Hulk" is handsome. More importantly, it takes a truly loving wife and husband to endure the hardships of frequent moves, and a couple that is dedicated and determined enough to do all the repairs necessary to improve the value of the home. If you are that special couple, and have those special talents, then this is probably your single best investment if you are on limited means.

Other than that, as far as being aggressively involved in this type of investment, my good friend, Al Alessandra, may have summed it up the best when he said, "I don't want to invest in it if I have to feed it, water it, or paint it."

Most rental income is going to come under the heading of "painting it." For most of us, that's more of a headache than we want to endure.

Wheeling and Dealing

Wheeling and dealing takes precedence in the real-estate market. I don't know all of the tricks of the trade, but there are a couple that you may be able to use. One of the most clever was recently made public in an interesting book, *The Greatest Real Estate Book in The World*, by Robert Stloukal. It's based on a little-used financial device known as a "pledge." Some people who don't have enough money for a downpayment get a third party to pledge a certain amount of money, which is placed in what is essentially an escrow account, and is kept *in lieu of the downpayment, not as the downpayment.* These funds belong to the third party as long as payments are made on the property being purchased.

Let's say you do have the money to put a downpayment of $20,000 on a house. Instead of using your $20,000, you give the $20,000 to a friend of yours, who then pledges it in place of your downpayment. The money in the pledge account will earn interest, currently somewhere in the area of 15%, and, hopefully, the value of your home will have appreciated over a five or six year time period to a point where there is at least that much additional equity, because of market inflation. So, say you bought a $90,000 house with a $20,000 pledge which is not a downpayment. The pledge is like a security deposit—that's all. Hopefully, after five years, the $90,000 house would be worth more than $110,000. You could refinance the house at that point. If you wanted to sell it, your only tied-up funds would have been the monthly payments you were making on the loan, as your downpayment funds were not used as a downpayment, but rather as a pledge drawing interest for you.

The Commission

Perhaps the most commonly used wheeling and dealing method is getting around paying brokerage commissions. Frankly, I prefer not to play the game that way. I think if some-one has spent the time to show me a piece of property, I am morally, if not legally, obligated to deal with that person. How-ever, that does not mean that I will not try to negotiate his or her commission rates. And, if something is consummated we can work out the brokerage commission arrangements so that the brokerage fees come due not out of the first downpayment monies, but, perhaps, sometime later, or even after the property is entirely paid for. You'll find most real estate people are amenable most of the time to some type of a commission deferral, if that is going to make or break the sale.

Other Kinds of Payment

Another neat, though morally questionable, technique that has been used in some parts of the country, is to use diamonds or bonds, or even corporate stock, as part of the downpayment, but not for the entire purchase price.

It works as follows: Let's say you have some land for sale that you would like to sell for $80,000. I come to you and say, "I don't have $80,00 in cash; however, I do have diamonds with an appraised value of $90,000." I then ask if you would be willing to exchange your land for my diamonds.

On the surface you've got a pretty good deal. You're getting more than you're asking for your property, and you have, what is supposedly, one of the best investments in the world. At least according to the "Apocalypse Now" crowd.

However, if you've already read the chapter on diamonds in this book, you know that I probably bought those $90,000 worth of diamonds for somewhere in the area of $40,000 to $45,000; perhaps even less. If the transaction is completed, I have bought your $80,000 piece of property for a cash investment of only $40,000 to $45,000. I could turn around and sell the property the next day, or at least wait for capital gains to take effect, and make a very hefty profit on my limited cash investment.

You can do the same thing with bonds. This can work particularly well, and perhaps in this case is more equitable to people who are about to retire. Let's say you find an elderly couple who want to sell some land. At this point in their lives, the couple's main concerns are security and income. You can offer them bonds that are paying a nice yearly rate of return that could, in many cases, be currently from 15% to 18%. Then when the bonds expire, let's say they expire in ten years, their market value might be up 20% to 30% above current price levels.

You approach the elderly couple and explain you don't have the cash to buy their property; however, you do have bonds that are valued *at* maturity at $100,000. You tell them you would like to give them your bonds in exchange for their property. If their property is worth somewhere in the $90,000 to $100,000 area, they may be interested. After all, they're getting a higher value than they're asking for, and people really fall for that. Also, they will be earning interest on the bonds while they wait for them to mature. They can borrow against the bonds if they need to get cash in a hurry.

What they most likely don't realize is that, currently, bonds are selling at a discount, and the bonds that mature for $1,000 each, you may have purchased in the market for $600 each. Thus, through the $100,000 bond you bought for $60,000, you acquired the property for 60 cents on the dollar.

Finally, another way of using the same approach is to buy discounted paper. Let's say someone has a note whose face value is $100,000. For whatever reason, the person needs cash and decides to sell that $100,000 note to you for $50,000. The note does have a market value of $100,000 when it comes due.

You use this note then as payment on the property. The person you are buying the property from may never know that you purchased the note at a discount. You just offer it as either collateral for a downpayment or for the entire purchase price, depending upon the value of the property in question.

If you are going to do any of these tricky financing maneuvers, and some of them are tricky, some perhaps even morally questionable, I think you will find it very advantageous not to quibble about the price with the seller. That's because my experience has shown a strange phenomenon takes place when you are willing to pay someone's price. If you don't quibble over price, most sellers completely drop their guard and common sense about the rest of the deal. Perhaps they figure that if you are willing to pay their price, you must not be too intelligent; or they're just tickled pink to have a figure they can brag about for the rest of their lives. In any event, most sellers will not pay close attention to the rest of the details—the financial arrangements—if they get their price. So let them have their price, but you have the terms; because terms can be more important than cash.

The Promissory Note Trick

Another neat purchasing trick Stloukal mentions is to tell the seller of an as-yet unbuilt house that you are perfectly willing to buy, but that you don't have the downpayment in cash; however, you say, you *do* have equity in your current house. You then ask the seller if he would be willing to take a nominal downpayment of, say, $500, and then take a promissory note for the balance of the downpayment, due upon the closing of your home.

In this situation, everyone is pleased. The seller has sold his house. You are happy, because your downpayment on the house is a mere $500, and you have time on your hands to do something about selling your own home, since the builder will not finish for a while.

The real twist here comes from the fact that when the agreements are entered into the house has yet to be built. Thus, when the house is built and completed, say ten to twelve months down the line, the house will have a higher value than was originally negotiated at today's date, because time does mean money, and in addition to even that, you have possible inflationary pressures. So the house that you may have contracted to buy for $80,000 may now have a market value of $86,000 to $87,000. You then have an option. You may take the house that you've purchased for $80,000 and turn it around and quickly sell it for $87,000. You've netted a $7,000 profit, and your only up-front cash investment was the nominal $500 to $1,000 downpayment.

Machiavellian Real Estate

I hope I have alerted you to the deviousness of investing in the real-estate market. It is no place for the "babe in the woods." City slickers and country boys alike are going to turn the "babe in the woods" every which way but loose, whenever they can. One of the best ways to protect yourself is to have good legal counsel or a good broker to help you, or at least to teach you some of the ins and outs of fancy dancing in the real estate market.

Re-Negotiating Your Mortgage

One of the easiest ways you can make some immediate savings, if you are a homeowner, is to re-negotiate, or alter, the terms of your current mortgage agreement. You can substantially reduce your house payments if you do the following:

Make two checks each month; one for the regular, full payment, the other just for the principal due the following month. As an example, on a $50,000 bank loan, at 13%, you'd have monthly payments of $553.10 for 360 months. The next month's principal payment, in this case, would be $11.56. Write on the back of the second check, "Endorsement thereof, acknowledged as payment for _____ (put in the principal payment date you are paying)."

In a year's time you will have actually made 24 house payments, paying interest and principal on twelve of them, and principal only on the other twelve. You will never have to pay the interest on the other twelve, as you have already prepaid them. In the first year, using the above example, you will save $6,480.00 in interest charges! Check the prepayment clauses in your note, but usually this method will work, and save you, literally, thousands of dollars a year.

If you haven't purchased a house yet, and are thinking of getting a mortgage, you may want to seriously consider the effect of a longer-term mortgage, which may allow you to borrow more money than a shorter-term mortgage, but is not in your best financial interests. As an example, if you were to buy a $75,000 house, put $15,000 down—you would then have a $60,000 mortgage. If that mortgage was for thirty years, at 13%, the interest over the full time-span of the mortgage would add up to $178,950. That's almost 140% more than the cost of the house itself. It's amazing what interest does, but you would end up paying $238,950, for a $75,000 house.

Let's say you decided to buy that $75,000 house, again with your $15,000 down, giving you a $60,000 mortgage at 13%. But this time, instead of financing it over thirty years, finance it over fifteen years. Your interest costs over the full term would be approximately $77,000; which means you would end up paying approximately $102,300 less in interest with the shorter-term loan. That's a savings of over 57%, and may actually be enough to allow you to buy a summer home someplace.

Here's the best way of seeing what happens; in the case of the house financed over fifteen years, at the end of ten years of payments, your equity in the home is $26,600. Whereas, in the thirty-year mortgage, at the end of ten years, your equity in the house is a measly $3,400.

The message is clear. If you can afford to do it, it's more to your advantage to keep your financing at as short a term as possible. The net effect of a shorter mortgage is going to be more dollars in your pocket, at the end of the mortgage, and more dollars more quickly in your house itself along the way.

Enjoying Real Estate

Jimmy Carter did everything but turn the lights off on civilization, and all that he could to make it fashionable to wear sackcloth. I believe we're going to see a change in that. People are willing to come out of the dark and enjoy their life-styles. That's going to mean larger homes, and nicer homes. Some of those homes will be nicer because of the technological changes, not only in energy production from fusion or solar, but also because of better insulation and better building designs. There's a future for the house of the future, and there's an even better future for real estate values.

Your purposes as a real estate investor should be to determine when demand is going to increase hungrily, not now, not in two or three months from now, but in three to six years from now; because that land is going to have the most spectacular increase in price.

Last Word

If there is a final word of real estate investment advice I can give you, it's that in addition to your scheming, you also have to do a good deal of reflecting on and contemplating the sociological and demigraphic changes that are going to take place in the area where you're interested in investing.

There is a story told in my family that one of my grandfathers, during the Depression, left Montana with a bunch of other Norwegians and went to California. He looked around California and decided no one would ever want to live in that particular part of California. It was too hot, it never snowed, you couldn't ski, so he came back to Montana. His other Norwegian buddies had the foresight to buy all the land they could in what's now known as Long Beach, California.

In the real estate business it's foresight that you get rewarded for, and I hope that this chapter has helped you to some degree develop your own personal foresight. I hope I've taught you something about real estate, but even more about how to perceive how things will be in the future.

6

Why the Most Money
Will Be in Entertainment,
or
Send Your Kids to
Ballet School—Not Harvard

Entertainment Megabucks

Believe it or nor, the most money to be made in the next ten years will not come from the canyons of Wall Street. Even the most spectacular Harvard graduates will not do as well as those who apply themselves to another little understood profession.

I'm talking about a profession where the average salary of its successful participants is well over one million dollars a year, where it's not unusual to see an "executive" in this industry earn that much or more in one month, one week or even frequently in one day.

I'm talking about riches that really are beyond most of our imaginations. Riches that certainly exceed what we are told J.R. and his buddies connive in oil-rich Texas, and riches far beyond the most successful Wall Street broker or lawyer. Best yet, the entrance fee, that is, the education to get involved in this business, is simple. It doesn't require four to eight years of arduous institutionalized study.

What I'm talking about is the entertainment business. It's clear there is more money to be made there than in any other legal business known to mankind.

This may strike you as unusual, but it is true, and it has been true, since the dawn of creation. And it is going to continue to be true for the rest of this decade, come boom or bust. I first dabbled in the entertainment business in 1971 when I was living in Carmel, California. I enjoy music of all types and having been brought up in Montana I particularly enjoy what has come to be known as Country-Western music. Of all the great Country-Western talents at that time, none were greater than Johnny Cash. I thought it would be profitable to bring Johnny Cash to the Monterey Peninsula during the Salinas Rodeo, one of the largest Rodeo events held in California and which had not then been supplying first-rate Country-Western entertainment.

119

I wrote to Johnny Cash and his agent and discovered a startling fact of life. Johnny Cash was willing to appear in Monterey, California, for a fee of $25,000.00 or 75% of the gross gate, whichever was the largest.

That was before Johnny Cash had truly become the superstar that he is now; and it wasn't for two or three shows—it was strictly a one-night stand. Our promotional costs would be absorbed by me; Cash got 75% of the gross, not the net.

As I said, I like Johnny Cash's music. But I didn't like it quite that much, so he never came to the Salinas Rodeo. But that did set my mind to thinking. It made me realize that more money is made in the entertainment business, by individuals, than in any other endeavor on Earth.

The Johnny Cash story is just the tip of the iceberg.

When considering entertainment, I place it into various categories, including sports, music, drama (which covers movies and television as well as the theater), dancing, and anything in general that makes life a little bit easier and more pleasurable for at least a few hours of our time.

In short, men and women want to be entertained, for which they're willing to pay substantial amounts of money.

Not a Bad Job If You Can Get It

Muhammad Ali perhaps proved this as well as anyone. In the fall of 1980 he fought Larry Holmes in Las Vegas in what proved to be a truly miserable fight. I was there. I believe our seats cost about $300 per person. We went expecting a truly remarkable athletic performance. And what we got instead was the humiliation of Muhammad Ali and nothing too spectacular either from Larry Holmes. What Ali *got*, however, was some $12 million, while Holmes picked up $6 million for less than 45 minutes of work.

Like they say, it's not a bad job if you can get it.

It seems you can pick up virtually any newspaper, turn to the sports section, and read about at least an athlete a day making $1 million a year or more. Mr. Dave Winfield now earns that tidy sum; his contract averages out to $10,000 per hit—that's hit, not home run.

The intellectuals have always pooh-poohed athletics and said the real money was to be made by going to college and getting either a liberal arts degree or learning a profession. It appears they were wrong all the time. In fact, there is more money made in chasing baseballs, footballs, and golf balls than in chasing clients or scientific theories.

But the truly big money in entertainment isn't in athletics. Paul McCartney, of Beatles fame, is living proof of how successful the entertainment business can be. The next time you see Paul McCartney or hear any of his songs or lyrics, I want you to think of $51 million. That's not what Paul McCartney is worth; no, $51 million is what Paul McCartney earns per year as an entertainer.

I've searched all the copies of *Fortune* and *Forbes* magazines to try to find a private entrepreneur or corporate giant whose yearly salary approaches what Paul McCartney earns, it's not to be found.

As I recall, Elton John brings in about $20 million a year, which still exceeds not only any corporate officer's salary, as published in *Forbes* and *Fortune*, but also exceeds the annual profits reported by most of those corporations.

Of course it could well be that Paul McCartney is the exception. So let us take the Beatle who has been considered the least musically inclined member of the group: Ringo. He did well banging on the drums with the Beatles, but you probably haven't heard much about him. However, a recent Associated Press article from London tells us Ringo is currently making almost $2½ million a year.

I think the point is well made. If you want *the* most successful and financially rewarding career for yourself or your children, it would not be in what we think of as the common high-money-making professions, doctor, lawyer, businessman. It would be in the entertainment business. And there are facets of the entertainment business that anyone can succeed at, even if he can't carry a tune in a bushel basket, paint, draw, dance or act.

Why Some People Get Paid More Than Others

There is an axiom in the stock market probably best expressed by my friend Richard Russell of the *Dow Theory Letter*. Dick has said that the biggest bonuses go to the investor who owns what no one else has. That's also true of the job market . . . to an extent.

When you stop and think about it, there is no way to explain why people are paid what they are paid. It simply does not make sense, at least on the surface. In traditional economic concepts, the more something is in demand, the higher the price will be; or, the greater supply there is of something, the lower the price will be. But when it comes to individual wage earnings, that traditional economic concept simply falls all apart.

There are very few people on planet Earth who wouldn't want to be another Paul McCartney. There are very few who don't want to succeed like a Muhammad Ali, a Dave Winfield, an Elton John, a Farrah Fawcett, a Tex Ritter, a Johnny Cash, a Rudolf Nuryev, or a Dan Rather. The supply of potential talent out there is great; everyone wants into this game. The other side of the equation is that one would expect the jobs that are the most demanding physically, and least rewarding socially, would pay a good salary so as to draw people. But that simply isn't so. The average janitor, perceived by many as in a demeaning social position, and certainly set upon physically, earns very little. The same goes for a ditch digger, a factory worker, and so on. Jobs that don't have much appeal, and even some that do require a good deal of skill, are still not high paying.

If we carry the analogy further, we see that people who are highly trained and may even have to go through four extra years of intensive training before entering the job market, like a lawyer or plumber, earn unequal amounts; and neither earns, on the average, as much as the super-stars of the entertainment world. To make it a fair analogy, you should compare the super-stars of, say, the plumbing business, the business of medicine, or that of law. Again, you find there is simply no comparison when you look at super-stars versus super-stars. Best yet, when the super-stars get old and start to lose their abilities, which happens more rapidly in athletics than any other field, they can start endorsing everything from Hertz

Rental cars to fishing poles and continue earning millions. Have you ever seen a commercial starring a retired plumber or lawyer?

The Ego-Exposure Factor

I wondered long and hard why this is true. Why does a bank president, who generally does not work as hard as many of his tellers, earn 20 to 30 times what tellers earn? Certainly he has more responsibility. But responsibility alone does not seem to be the clue; what responsibility does Elton John or Johnny Carson have?

My studies have led me to believe that the unknown factor **X** of personal rewards, in terms of salaries, comes not from the work one does, nor from the type of work one does; and in many cases not even the ability of the worker or the performance of the work itself, but from the amount of exposure of one's ego.

There it is! In a nutshell it seems to go like this: the more you must expose your ego in your job, the greater your reward is going to be. And this does fit classic economics, which says the greater risk there is, the greater reward there shall be.

There is virtually little risk to one's ego cleaning floors in Safeway after store hours. But there is great risk to one's ego in signing a stockholders' report or performing in front of a crowd, because the loves, hates, and prejudices of stockholders or of a crowd are fickle and at any moment can change. When this happens you go instantly from super-star to super-nothing. We see it happen all the time. That's what trivia is based on, all the washed-out super-stars of previous generations.

That also explains why corporate treasurers, or even corporate lawyers and personnel recruiting officers, who may be much more important to a corporation than its president or chairman of the board, don't receive even close to the remuneration they get. The person who takes the most total personal risk, which of course falls on his shoulders, exposing his self or ego to destruction, is the one that's going to end up with the most bucks at the end of the month.

The same theory applies to athletics, both conceptually as well as *on a time frame*. For instance, quarterbacks get paid more than centers. After all, you probably can't name more than two or three famous college or professional centers, yet you probably *can* name several handfuls of quarterbacks. Quarterbacks are the ones we watch suffer the mistakes and enjoy the triumphs. But even a quarterback's exposure to ego risk isn't based on just one game. It may be based on a season's performance or even the performance over two or three years, if the team is building or regenerating phase. And that's probably why quarterbacks' salaries are not as extreme as those of athletes whose entire livelihood can be made or destroyed in one performance.

How to Make the Ego Factor Work for You

Now you know why Sugar Ray Leonard and Roberto Duran can each bring down a cool $8 million in one evening: simply because in those brief 45 to 90 minutes virtually their entire being is exposed; they're putting it all on the line. That appears to be why they are rewarded as well as they are. The more you have to risk, the greater the rewards; which is why the heavyweight champ, "The Champion of the World," earns more than the bantamweight champ, who is almost always a better boxer.

Obviously, we the public enjoy seeing professional athletes, or any professional people, entertain us, and we do appreciate the quality and caliber of their service to us. However, considering all of the entertainment fields, I think you'll find that ego risk is what is going to bring you the greatest reward. This can be useful to you if you are interested in getting into the entertainment business and getting to where the big bucks really are. If you're going to play in a 40-piece band on the Lawrence Welk Show, you're not going to make the money that Lawrence Welk does. After all, if you play off-key, probably no one else is going to notice except the other musicians next to you. But if the entire band plays off-key, the band members can individually get other jobs or regroup, but Lawrence Welk is washed up.

How to Be in The Entertainment
Business—Even If You Can't Carry a Tune

You may have been thinking that this chapter isn't terribly pertinent to you. After all, you're not about to go to acting school, don't disco, and can't tell one note from the other.

Don't worry. There is a phase of American business that operates on the same rules that the entertainment business does; that operates and succeeds *because of* the entertainment business.

I think that over the next ten years, you are going to see this loose-knit agglomeration we call the entertainment industry become the single largest-growing industry in the United States of America. What I am talking about is the "industry" of entertainment products. As the machine age has become more and more a part of our lives, and our lives become more and more technological, I think you're going to see products, machines of one form or another, becoming our entertainment to a very great extent.

It's already begun. It began, perhaps, 40 years ago with the pinball machines, which have now advanced to home game sets where you can shoot astroids out of the sky on your television, or play chess with Boris, a pre-programmed chess master. But it goes beyond just the games of entertainment; it goes to products that are entertaining.

What Hot Tubs And Calculator Watches
Have in Common

I think the underlying success of hot tubs, calculator watches, and transistor radios all gets back to entertainment. I seriously doubt if there is anyone who really needs a hot tub in his home, yet hot tubs are one of the best selling items for new houses. And it's for certain that we don't also need to have watches that also have calculators on them. But again, they continue to be a big-selling item. These are items that do have some utilitarian value, it is true. But by and large their greatest value comes from entertaining us in one fashion or another, from providing enjoyment for our leisure moments.

You can see this at work even in the restaurant business. The most successful restaurants of the tail end of the '70s have been "theme" restaurants, restaurants that are designed with a particular theme in mind. Whether it is Trader Vic's, with all the beauty and serenity of the Polynesian Islands or the extremely successful Victoria Stations, with the feel of the by-gone era of railroads, "theme" restaurants have been much more successful than those that simply serve food.

One of the best marketing tips I have ever received was given to me by a fellow who said: "People like to be romanced." The entertainment business proves that every single day. The LED watch bonanza is a good case in point. For many, many years people had worn watches with hour, minute and second hands, but when the LED crystals came out, they threw those watches away and bought the new LED watches by the hundreds of thousands. Both told time with about the same degree of accuracy. But one was new. It was entertaining; it did things that previous watches didn't do. It could function as a stop watch, a calendar, an alarm clock and had what were perceived as advantages. And they did have, but beyond those advantages they offered a form of entertainment to the wearer.

I'm also predicting we're going to see the same or a similar trend take place in the auto industry. Due to the energy crisis, cars in America have become very austere and mundane. Within the next five years, we're going to see someone start making cars that are fun, that are entertaining and perhaps even exciting. Those are the cars that are going to sell the most and it is that car company whose stock you are going to want to purchase.

How to Make a Fortune in Entertainment Publishing

The entertainment business has proliferated in the publishing industry as well. Virtually everyone in America is exposed to the publishing industry: whether it's electronic or graphic publishing, we're all exposed to books, newspapers, radio, and television, perhaps hundreds of times each day. This entire group falls into what I classify as the entertainment industry and should feature some of your best investment potentials for starting your own business.

In fact, here is a sure-fire formula for making yourself wealthy. All you need to do is find some burgeoning group of people that has a unique and specialized interest; then publish a magazine or newspaper for that group of people.

About 15 years ago, those of us who were into jogging had no way to communicate with each other or find out what was taking place within the recreational pursuit of jogging. The first few issues were meager and done off a mimeograph, but ultimately, a magazine known as *Runners' World* was created and now grosses more than $20 million per year in advertising and subscription revenues. Who would have thought fifteen years ago there was a fortune to be made telling those nuts running around the country in sweatsuits where the races were going to be held next month? Very few people—but the formula worked.

Others made millions of dollars when the CB radio craze captured America's interest in specialized CB radio magazines or books. Again, there was a unique interest, and though the product had been on the scene for a long time, it suddenly caught hold. While there was money made in selling the CB products, the easiest and best money was made simply publishing information about the CB products, or providing information/entertainment about the product item.

The same thing holds true of the recreational vehicle industry. There have been millions of dollars made, and lost, in the production and manufacture of recreational vehicles, such as campers and motor homes. But money was only made by those who put together publications for this new interest group in America.

So if you want to really hit it big yourself, I would suggest you keep your eyes and ears tuned to what's happening with the public and try to find one of these about-to-skyrocket special-interest groups, and become a publisher for that industry. *You* could start with a magazine or news-letter for the home computer craze.

Perhaps the easiest way to get into this business is simply to notice what you yourself are doing. Are you looking at new products? Are you and others getting heavily involved in a new activity or pastime, but find there is no official trade publication or information source on the subject? If you find that, you will have found yourself a gold mine.

The Travel Gambit

Perhaps the greatest growth in the entertainment industry is going to come from the entertainment provided to us in travel. I think you're going to see people making millions and millions and millions of dollars by providing transportation to recreation and vacation spots. And we're going to see places that were not previously thought of as being vacation areas become vacation areas as the Hawaii's of the world become overcrowded and no longer "in." The people I know who have taken good advantage of this trend have ranged from those who have put together entertainment complexes, ranging from motels in traditional tourist towns, such as Lake Placid, New York, to those who have put together Holiday Inns or even more luxurious entertainment complexes with convention centers, golf ranges, tennis courts, etc. All have done very well on mankind's desire to get away from home, to escape the mundane and have an experience in the art of living.

Fortunately for the average investor, a quick trip to your stockbroker's office will expose you to numerous corporations that are already making good profits in the entertainment business. They run the gamut from Bally Manufacturing (a large manufacturer of gambling equipment) to Holiday Inns of America.

A very good example of my sure-fire way to make a million dollars within the travel and entertainment industries is an interesting newsletter called *Hideaway Report*, P.O. Box 66, Fairfax Station, VA 22039. The editor, Andy Harper, simply travels around the world to very enjoyable resorts and then writes about them once a month, sending his letter of advice to clients. I don't know how many subscribers Andy has, but he appears to be making a very enjoyable and comfortable living by following today's "golden rule formula" of being the communicator for a special interest.

Let me end this chapter by saying that when it comes to any investment decision during the '80s, or '90s for that matter, I suggest you think in terms of entertainment. Is a product entertaining; does a corporation provide an entertaining service; what are the new trends in entertainment? A mass of fortunes were made when we shifted from newspapers to radios to television, and then as television spread out into Beta and VHS home recorder sets for the television. More fortunes were made as the recording industry went from records to cassettes and cartridge tapes.

Learning About Entertainment

Instead of reading the *Wall Street Journal*, you may want to consider a subscription to *Variety*, the bible of the entertainment industry. As we become more electronically oriented, I would pay very close attention to the evolution of electronic entertainment. The first company to come out with the wide or giant screen home television sets made money hand over fist. For sure, we are going to see more changes and improvements in the way electronic entertainment is provided for us, and I hope you'll be there to take advantage of those unique investment opportunities.

If you can ever buy stock in an entertainer, as did the group of Clover Leaf investors when they purchased former-World-Heavyweight Joe Frazier's contract, do it. If you have a good entertainer, one who is willing to undergo the exposure and ego-risk factors I've discussed, you have a potential winner.

So forget about gold, to some degree forget about financial statements and profit and loss ratios, and focus in on the emerging trends of entertainment of the '80s and '90s. Because today's entertainers are not like little Tommy Tucker, who couldn't pay for his supper. They not only can pay for the supper, they can probably buy the restaurant as well.

7

High-Yield Investing—
The Art of Getting the Most
With the Least Risk

Making a Lot With Little Aggravation

I wrote my first article on "High-Yield Investing" in 1966. At that time I had discovered some investments that, in my opinion, were safe and secure, and yielded between 8% and 10%. I thought that my research brilliance would be rewarded and investors would be tremendously pleased with having security and a high yield.

I received one of the shocks of my life when I found out that a good many people thought that the article was either misleading, or downright dishonest. Many, many people said it was virtually impossible to earn 10% on your money on anything but an extremely risky investment.

Now that we can look back on the '70s and see Government Bonds yielding 18% to 19%, the Prime Rate at over 20%, and banks now paying 16% to 17%, perhaps I am rewarded with the last laugh after all.

Market Child's Play

The point can be made that what at one time may seem like an astronomical interest rate—say 8% to 10%—a little later on may seem like child's play. Additionally, what may seem like an astronomical rate in one country, may seem like child's play in yet another country. At the time my research was done and we found some investments yielding 8% to 10% on a conservative basis in the United States, there were investments in foreign countries that would be yielding all the way up to 18%, with just as much security. Now the tables have been reversed. There are several countries right now, where the bank rates are substantially less than one half of the bank interest rates in this country.

131

The Compensating Balance Gambit

Suffice it to say, however, that regardless of how bad economic conditions are, you're always going to be able to find, if you do your homework, some conservative investments that have higher yields than others. To my way of thinking, one of the greatest tricks that's ever been played on the American investor, and, sadly enough, on the working men and women of America, has been perpetrated by the financial institutions of this country. They spend millions of dollars on advertising each year in an effort to solicit funds. But the truth of the matter is, one can increase his returns anywhere from 25% to 30% per year by ignoring those ads, and finding equally reliable sources for his money. There is one way, however, that you can get a substantial return on your investment in a bank account that I would like to share with you. The method is based on compensating balances. If you have done any substantial borrowing from a bank, you may have been asked by the bank to keep a certain amount of your money on deposit; if someone borrows $100,000, for example, the bank may ask him to keep $20,000 on deposit. The bank then uses this money to hypothecate, creating even more money which it can then lend out to other people.

The problem is that the borrower has $20,000 of his $100,000 frozen in the bank. It's good for the bank, but not good for the borrower. Worse yet, he's not drawing any interest on the funds.

You, as an investor, can profit from this situation, if you are on good terms with your bank. You do this by telling the person who has borrowed the money from the bank that you will put up the compensating balance, let's say the $20,000; which allows him to use the full $100,000 in his own business. You will provide the $20,000 at, say, 10% interest. That's very attractive to the borrower, because he can't borrow that $20,000 that cheaply from the bank, as things stand. Your next maneuver is to go to the banker and say you are willing to put up either Treasury Bills or your savings account book in place of the borrower's compensating balance. That should satisfy the banker, because he still has your dollars to hypothecate on.

You can see, then, you are earning interest from both parties.

The bank savings, pass-book, or Treasury Bills are paying you current rates, perhaps as high as 15%, and you are getting 10% from the person whose compensating balance you have released. Thus, your net yield on the investment is 25%!

Cautionary Words on the Compensating Balance Gambit

If you do this, you have to make certain that your compensating balance is not used as collateral for the $100,000 loan that the borrower has taken out; or, if it is to be used as collateral: that 1) you get a substantially higher rate of return, and 2) you have your investment protected with the borrower so, if there is a default, you have some recourse.

This is a neat trick. It can be performed in almost any banking community, regardless of size. There are always some borrowers who have compensating balances, and it's very nice to keep your money in the bank, drawing interest from both parties.

High-Yield Bonds

Another way of participating in high-yield investing is to buy bonds. There are some Government Bonds that currently have a very high yield. At times, given the cyclical phenomenon of the interest-rate markets, these bond yields are extremely high. If you can lock in on those high yields on a longer term, say two to five years, during a time when you believe interest rates are going down, as I believe is going to occur in the '80s, you're going to have a locked-in yield that will be substantially higher than yields that will be available to your later on.

You can do this with Corporate Bonds or you may do it with U.S. Government Bonds. The drawback, of course, is that you are really tied into that bond until it matures if you want to get the rate of interest shown. If you get out of the bond earlier, since the price may have gone down even lower than your purchase price, you may actually lose money on the transaction. If, however, you do hold onto the bond until it reaches maturation and the bond is offered by a company or government that is sound, stable and can make good on the bond obligation, you will have received a higher rate of interest than if you'd placed those same funds in a bank account. Most bank savings accounts don't pay as much interest rate as the bonds do, after all, and those interest rates offered by banks and savings and loans do move up and down—most likely down over the next few years.

Bond to Bank: How to Make an Easy Killing

From time to time, you may find bonds yielding a higher rate of return than what a bank will charge you to borrow money. If such a situation exists, you have an excellent opportunity to increase your true yield. Let's look at an example. Say there was a bond yielding 18% and bank rates dropped to the point where you could borrow money for 15%; and that you have, for illustrative purposes, $100,000 to invest. You can buy $100,000 of the bonds, yielding the 18%, take those bonds to the bank and borrow $50,000. You borrow $50,000 at 15%, which means you would be paying $7,500 a year in interest. You take the $50,000 and buy more of the 18% bonds. Your net return would be $9,000 a year, minus the $7,500 a year you are paying. This will net you an increase of $1,500 a year. Your true return, then, will be the $18,000 from your first $100,000 bonds, plus $1,500 for total return of $19,500; as opposed to the return, without the financing, of $18,000. Your true income, then, is 8% higher by financing the bonds through the bank than if you had just bought $100,000 worth of these bonds. This technique can be applied to virtually any investment. In any solid investment, whenever you can borrow money for less than what *you* can charge to lend it out to someone else, it may be advisable to borrow that money and lend it out to that other party, whether it's through bonds, compensating balance bank accounts or money funds. This used to be an easier maneuver to pull off than it is now. With the high interest rate we've seen recently, it has been a little difficult.

However, my crystal ball indicates that bank account rates are going to come down substantially. Yet we should see some of the rates stay at relatively high levels; so we may see this opportunity open up in the first part of the '80s for conservative investors. If stocks and commodities or real estate are not your cup of tea and you want something with less fluctuation, you should pay very close attention to some of these opportunities. Any of the conservative, high-yield investment programs mentioned in this chapter should provide an opportunity of keeping your investment marginal while increasing your yields.

Easy Money Funds

One of the major monetary developments of the '70s is the advent of the "money funds." As most everyone now knows, certain investment advisors formed pools where they would take an investor's money and purchase Treasury Bills, Ginnie Maes, Treasury Bonds, or other high-yielding government or corporate obligations. Instead of investing the money in stocks, they simply invested the money in the highest-yielding paper that they could find, charged their management fees, and passed on the rest of these terrific high yields to their investors. That has virtually changed the investment market. It's made the banks much more competitive. It has actually changed the way we now look at the money currently in circulation. I realize the money funds will be with us for a good while to come, and, by and large, are the very best investment for the average person seeking a high return. They usually provide a higher return than the banks or savings and loans. They have great liquidity. You can get in and out of them almost instantaneously.

How To Make At Least $1,000 . . . Today

There is a way you can use the Money Funds to make an immediate and substantial amount of money, yes, today, if you happen to have insurance policies that you took out ten, fifteen or more years ago.

The vast majority of those policies give you the right, as a policy owner, to borrow against the policy itself.

A good number of Americans do have paid-up policies— anywhere from $10,000 to $100,000 of paid-up life insurance. You may be one of the lucky people who made payments on such a life insurance policy in the 1950s or 1960s. If so, check to see if you can borrow against your policy; because, most likely, you'll be able to borrow against your policy at anywhere from an interest rate of 2% to, in some cases, 7% or 8%.

What an opportunity that presents for those who have paid-up policies, or paid-in-part policies! Imagine, you can borrow your $10,000, $20,000 or more at, let's say, 5% rate of interest which is guaranteed to you in your policy. So, go right ahead and do that. Call up your insurance company and borrow the money today, because you can turn right around and take the money you borrowed at, say 5%, and put it in a Money Fund, which is currently going to earn you somewhere in the area of 17% or 18%.

Let's say that you have a paid-up policy of $10,000, and you will be paying 5% interest, or $500 per year on the money you are borrowing from the insurance company. That's your cost of doing business, the $500 you are going to have to pay back, in addition to the $10,000 principal. But, if you take that principal and put it in a Money Fund, or other investments you'll learn about in this chapter, paying 18%, you will be receiving an income of $1,800 from that investment. Deduct the $500 interest fee from borrowing the money from the insurance company, and you are going to make yourself a hefty $1,500 per year; that's not too shabby, considering that you have virtually no risk if you are placing your money in T-Bills, Money Funds or even, in some cases, in bank or savings and loan accounts that are now paying high rates of interest.

This is the very first investment pointer that I make to anyone with whom I talk. This is money that you should be earning right now but aren't, because you simply haven't thought about the insurance policy and what you can do with that loan. It is probably the best "sure-fire" way, the average person can pick up an immediate $1,000 or more from simply moving one piece of paper here and another piece of paper over there.

Rob A Bank?

A few years ago there were several books flooding the markets, saying that there was a way of earning interest on bank account money that was almost as profitable as robbing a bank without a gun. What the central thesis behind the books' concept was is that you could open an account with a bank that was paying interest on checking accounts, and then use those checks to float money into savings-and-loan associations which would pay you interest from the first of the month as long as the deposit was made by the 10th of the month. If one were adroit enough to do this with several savings and loans and different bank accounts, there would be a slight possibility that you might be able to bump up your interest earnings from, perhaps, 7%, all the way up to 9% to 12%.

That could be done, and can still be done; but, to my way of thinking, although it is not illegal, it is a bit questionable; because one, essentially ends up kiting checks. While that is probably something that everyone in America has done at one time or another; still it's a pretty shaky way of doing business. I would prefer to find things that inherently are going to pay a high rate of interest, and not have to worry about whether my checks are clearing in time, and whether I'm getting a check from the bank to the savings-and-loan on the correct date. There is simply too much worry for the small amount of extra interest that one is going to pick up.

Beating the Bond Market

Many people have the misconception that the Bond market is a safe place to be. It represents a safe investment if, and only if, one does not try to trade the market. If you simply sit on a Bond until it matures, and the Bond is one that will be redeemed— paid off—by a corporation or government, you're not going to lose any money. But, if you buy a Bond, especially if you buy it on margin and it drops, and you have to come up with additional money that you don't have, you will have to sell your Bonds and take a loss.

Therefore, the best way to play the Bond market is not to play it, in terms of trading; but, simply, to invest in it. If you are going to do that, you should take a look at the *Wall Street Journal* to see what Bonds are currently paying. You will find there are two listings of Bonds in the Journal. One is under Government

Agency and Miscellaneous Securities; and one is under the Commercial Bond Market itself. Currently, in the Government Agency and Miscellaneous Securities Bonds, there are Government Bonds yielding up to 18%. Further, the interest on many of these receive favorable tax treatment. Here are just some current examples of the types of interest you can get from Bond markets guaranteed by the government: The "Fannie Maes," or F.N.M.A., Bonds of September, 1981, are currently yielding 15.72%; Federal Farm Credit Notes, which receive substantial preference when tax time comes, are currently yielding 15.7% for the August, 1981, Notes, and 15.4% for the March, 1982, Notes. If you are willing to take a chance with the World Bank Bonds, you can currently get 18.5% on several of their Notes.

If you then flip a few pages ahead in your *Wall Street Journal*, you will see the listing of the New York Exchange Bonds. They are listed by the name of the Bond, the year that it expires, and the current yield it is paying. You might want to peruse the list and examine the current yields; you'll be amazed to see what some of America's major corporations are paying for interest. As an example, I would like to point out that Chrysler Bonds are paying anywhere from 17% to 18% interest, which isn't bad when you consider that, to an extent, they are guaranteed by the Federal Government. Gulf Resources are paying 16%, Gulf Oil is paying 16%, and GELCO is paying 17% on notes that come due in 1999.

Pacific Telephone and Telegraph Notes of 2020 are yielding 16%; but that's a little bit too long for me. Of course, you would be receiving interest payments on your Bond along the way. And if the Bond goes up in price, you will make even more money. There are several Bonds on the American Stock Exchange List that are also paying 17% to 18%.

One thing is certain; if you are interested in receiving the highest possible yield, you should find out as much as you can about the Bond market. There are some excellent opportunities arising from time to time that will give you high rates of interest, while, at the same time, offering the safety of investing in major corporations, such as utilities, manufacturers and, yes, even the computer companies.

Banking Abroad For Higher Rates

While in search of higher interest rates, one should not over-look banks in foreign countries. Many of these banks have systems that (when it comes to redeeming people's savings) are actually sounder than American banks and even pay higher rates of interest than we are currently seeing in this country.

This is the type of situation you have to monitor continually. There are two factors to look at. One is the security. What is the possibility of the country's currency being devalued, as the Mexican peso was a few years ago? The interest rate that one could receive from banks in Mexico at that time was approximately 10 to 12 percentage points higher than was being received here. That was fine if you got your money out before the devaluation, but if you kept your money in pesos during the devaluation, you were clobbered.

The other factor you have to monitor is the interest rates. They will vary from one country to another and from time period to time period. Currently, interest rates in England are higher than they are in America, and we've seen that flip-flop both ways. Interest rates are lower in Germany than they are in America, and about the same in Switzerland as in the United States. Frequently we have seen lower rates in Switzerland than here: that is pretty much the yo-yo effect again. You have to watch the markets carefully. But the astute person, who does watch the markets carefully (that is much easier to do if you live in, say, New York, Chicago, Los Angeles, Atlanta, Miami, Houston, and the other international cities in this country), can follow what's taking place in foreign banks, and increase his returns rather dramatically.

In some foreign countries, banks are currently paying anywhere from 20% to 30% rates of interest, but inflation in those countries is usually running 60% to 100% (most notably Argentina or Israel). I doubt that one would want to make serious investments in banks of those countries because of the fear of devaluation, if not the collapse of the financial community there.

I remember well when I was living in Beirut, Lebanon, prior to the war breaking out, that some banks and financial institutions were paying 25% to 30% on savings accounts. The problem, of course, was that everyone knew there was the potential for a war. When it came, the financial community simply collapsed. Banks pulled out, money was pulled out, people didn't get their money, some people got money that didn't belong to them. The financial community was simply in a state of turmoil. You obviously don't want to be in the midst of that type of situation.

How You Can Be the Banker and Earn 20%–30% Interest

It's done on a rather quiet and limited basis, but throughout the country many people are assuming the roll of banker in their own community, and making an easy 20% to 30% each and every year on their money with a high degree of security, and, at the same time, flexibility.

The way this is done is as follows: there is a market in virtually every community, in every country, in every state, of people who are willing to sell Real Estate Notes. Say you sold me a house for $50,000. I put down a downpayment of, perhaps, $20,000; you are then holding a Note for $30,000. You would, of course, like to have your $30,000 now, instead of receiving the money over a long time period.

As a matter of fact, you would like to have that $30,000 so badly now that you would discount the $30,000 Note, and sell it to a third party for, say, $20,000. Thus, the person who buys the discounted Note not only receives the original interest that I guaranteed I would pay to you, but also receives the amount the Note had been discounted.

In this case, if it is discounted $10,000, you will pick up an additional 33% interest over whatever time period the Note is made for. Thus, let's say the Note was carrying 10% yearly interest over five years. The person who purchased the discount Note for $20,000 would, in fact, get 10% interest on $30,000, or $3,000 a year there, and would, of course, pick up the full amount of the Note after five years. Thus, he would pick up a gross of $10,000, and his $3,000 payment for each of the five years would be approximately $15,000, meaning his net on the net amount of income from the Note was $25,000. The Note was held for a five year time period, and the return, as you can see, is rather spectacular.

You're not going to find Notes as spectacular as these all the time, but they are out there. They are usually advertised in the classified sections of major newspapers. If you live in the Seattle area, certainly the *Seattle Times* is going to show you where these discount Notes are, as will the *San Francisco Chronicle*, the *Los Angeles Times*, the *Salt Lake City Tribune*, any of the major Chicago papers, the *Denver Post*, any of the papers in Dallas, Fort Worth, Houston, and on it goes across the country. Keep your eye peeled, and you will see classified ads from people who want to sell their Notes, some at substantial discounts. This is certainly one of the better ways of getting a high yield with a good degree of safety on your money. You've got to remember that you are, in fact, playing the roll of a banker. That means you're going to have to do some leg work and some credit checks on your own. You're going to want to make certain of three things: first, you're going to want to make certain that the person has the ability of pay off the Note; second, in the event the person does not have the ability to pay off the Note, you'll need to have some type of collateral, an interest in the property that will more than pay off your Note; and third, you should run the numbers on the Note you are going to buy, so you know exactly what the rate of return will be. All too often people buy Notes, but look only at the discount and not the number of years they are going to be holding the Note. Thus, they fail to realize the type of return they will actually be getting.

I cannot overstate, however, the importance of playing the role of the banker and doing your homework. You have to make certain *yourself* that you will get your money. Instead of going into great lengths with it here, I would simply suggest that you read a few books on credit in your local library. They are going to tell you the primary things you will want to look for, such as a person's payment habits, current income, other debt obligations, and then, of course, to see if the property has enough value to pay off the Note in the event the person is unable to himself.

The Number One Way to High Yield Returns

An exciting opportunity has developed in California for people interested in extraordinarily high rates of returns. This has occurred because the state of California has different laws on second mortgages than the majority of states. Instead of second mortgages, California has Second Deeds of Trust. The basic difference between a Second Deed of Trust and a second mortgage is that it is much easier to foreclose on a Second Deed of Trust. For that very reason there is an extremely small rate of foreclosure on Second Trust Deeds in the state of California.

This translates into investment security. It's estimated that last year fifty to sixty thousand people in California went to private mortgage loan brokers who, for a fee, find lenders—perhaps someone like you—willing to lend on a Second Deed of Trust.

These loan brokers usually charge anywhere from four to eight percentage points for arranging the loan, with some charging up to 15%. Nonetheless, because property values in California have appreciated so much, it has become a popular way of borrowing money.

Let's say you're living in California. You bought a house for $30,000. The house may now well be worth $100,000. Thus, you can take out a Second Deed of Trust on the house for $50,000 or even $60,000. Foreclosures in California have been extremely rare. In fact, in 1980, less than .05 of the outstanding Second Trust Deeds in California went into foreclosure status. In 1978, only 127 Second Trust Deeds were foreclosed on.

As I said, there is a reason for this. It's because foreclosing is so easy to do in California. Thus in California you get a borrower more concerned about making his payments than you would find in other states.

Now, if you are in California or any other state and are lending your money to a savings-and-loan association which is paying you anywhere from 7% to 10% on the money, you have to remember that what they are doing is lending your money into the market place by itself. In other words, they are acting as an agent for you, and, of course, they are getting paid quite handsomely for that. You can become your own banker or savings-

and-loan director by investing in Second Deeds of Trust in California.

What You Want in Second Deeds of Trust

There's a wide range of advertisers with Second Deeds of Trust for sale in California. You, of course, are making a loan directly to an individual. You are not making it to a financial institution. However, I think we are going to see a change here; someone is going to put together a mutual-type fund for Second Trust Deeds in California. He is going to make a killing on that. He is going to take away all of the money that has gone into the Money Funds, because the Money Funds cannot compete with the high rate of return offered by Second Deeds of Trust. I have advised people to invest in Second Deeds of Trust in California since the late '60s, and everyone has been extremely pleased with the results.

It is not just an anomaly that a small percentage of these loans are being pre-paid. Bonded Home Loans Company, in Los Angeles, said, in a recent interview, that 83 or 100 Trust Deeds that they had were pre-paid, which increased the investor's yields almost two percentage points. To me this represents the finest combination of safety and high-yield investing that I have been able to isolate in this country. It is easy. The average person can do it. The average person can understand it.

A couple of pointers that you need to know before entering the Second Deed of Trust market are similar to those in buying discounted Notes. You obviously have to make certain that the person you are lending the money to has the ability to pay. What you are looking for, then, is a financial statement on that person, to see what his total income is—both him and his wife, if he is married—and what his total bills are. You should also check to see if he has been slow to pay in previous financial commitments. If he has, you don't want to touch him; he'll probably be slow to pay with you. You want a responsible individual who makes his payments on time. You also want to see what his total current payments are, to make certain he has the money. If you subtract total current obligations that he has from income, you'll have an idea whether he'll have enough money to pay off the money he is borrowing from you.

Protect Yourself

Even more important would be to make certain that you are well protected, in the event he defaults on the Note. The best way of doing this is to have an appraised value on the property. Let's say the house appraises at $100,000. Then find out what the First Mortgage is. If the First Mortgage is for, say, $30,000, then you could make a Second Mortgage of $40,000, $50,000 or even $60,000. But, obviously, if you were to make a Second Mortgage for, say, $100,000, you would not have any equity protection in the house. In the event the house had to be sold to pay off both the First and the Second Mortgage, the sale of the house would net, maybe, between $90,000 and $100,000. The First Mortgage is paid off first, of course, and they get their $30,000 from the $90,000 proceeds from the house. The rest of the money would go to you on the Second Deed of Trust, but that would not be enough to cover the original amount you advanced.

For that reason, you must make certain that the combination of the First Deed of Trust and Second Deed of Trust, the money you are lending, is not greater than the total appraised value of the property. I would also be a little leery to have both the First and Second Deed of Trust equal the appraised value, because my experience has been that many homes do not sell for the appraised value. They sell for anywhere from the appraised value to 10% less than the appraised value. The most secure Second Deed of Trust play you could make would be one where both the First and Second Deed of Trust values represent less than 90% of the appraised value of the house or on whatever property it is you are lending money for. If you can find that situation, you really have an ideal high-yield investment opportunity.

Sources of Information

Without any doubt, the very best Second Deed of Trust business in California is "Reliable Mortgage." It would be your very best contact source for information and the possibility of having it acquire Second Deeds of Trust for you to invest in.

I have personally recommended the firm of Norman B. Lopes, Inc. 4000 Morepark Avenue, Suite 116, San Jose, CA 95117, to investors; and, in fact, have even recommended it to members of my immediate family, and would suggest you contact, if you are interested in this type of high-yield investing, John Sheffield.

While not as large a firm as Reliable Mortgage, I have the utmost confidence in their abilities to protect their investors; while, at the same time, helping us bring in the highest rate of return.

8

How to Get Aboard the Right Train Early

Why "Fads" Mean Money

Investment opportunities arise from economic or social change. Hence, the astute investor is constantly monitoring trends to see if he can't detect changes and shifts in economic data, whether it's consumer interest and demand, desires, or the direction of general businesses. Perhaps the real trick to virtually every investment, regardless of its nature—from real estate to commodities, or from diamonds to dehydrated foods—is to get in early, before the crowd, and ride the trend as long as you can, or at least until it appears the trend is starting to dissipate.

It may come as a surprise to you, but there have been substantial fortunes made and, in fact, some people make their entire living just chasing "fads." They'll notice that something is getting popular, say *Star Wars*, and will either have the licensing rights or buy the rights to sell Star Wars t-shirts, Star Wars thermos jugs, lunch boxes, cassette tapes, comic books, etc. Once they see that fad start fading, they'll switch to a new fad, which may be the *Shogun* fad, the Dallas Cowboys, yo-yo's, hula hoops, the death of John Lennon, or the birth of sextuplets. Whatever it is, there are people whom we more commonly know as promoters, who do nothing other than continually monitor trends and try to get aboard what they think is a viable trend early with the desired items.

How to Monitor Investment Possibilities

There are several ways of monitoring these changes in the investment world that I would like to recommend. The first one is that you simply monitor what people are doing. That means you must be aware, more alert. Listen to what your friends are doing, what changes are coming about in their lives. The CB radio fad was a good case in point. Many of us had friends who started getting into the CB lingo, and they told us a little bit about it. The vast majority of us just sat there and listened. We didn't do anything about it, even though that change in consumer behavior did account for substantial investment opportunity.

I remember, in the late '60s and early '70s, getting aboard the gold and silver investment fad. I got aboard the train very early, fortunately, because I noticed that quite a few people were paying more attention to silver and gold than they had in the past. Then, when I did my own research, of course, I found good evidence for the lasting power of that trend. I hope I am now correct in anticipating the reversal in the gold and silver markets. I believe that is, perhaps, the largest contribution of this particular book.

Monitoring Political Change

It goes beyond the investment circles as well. It is wise, in my opinion, to notice what is happening in the political arena, to see who the political up-and-comers are, and see whether you can't help in some way, if through a political contribution or licking stamps or knocking on doors. Join up with an up-and-coming political figure, and back him to the hilt as he grows more popular in the political circle. Certainly the people who got aboard the Jimmy Carter bandwagon early, or the Ronald Reagan bandwagon early, have profited, perhaps not in terms of dollars, but in terms of influence, power, and certainly in terms of making meaningful use of their time.

Paying Attention to What Different People Are Doing

In paying attention to people, I trust you will pay attention to people not only of your social and age set, but also, to those older and younger than you. Obviously, most of the fads catch on with younger people, whether it's designer jeans, or *Star Wars*, but the elderly, too, have some effect: note the burgeoning number of retirement homes and nursing centers. All of us, at all levels of society, go through changes and improvements in our life-styles, and you need to be on your toes to detect the changes at virtually all levels of human interaction. It is, of course, easier to notice what is happening in your own set, whether it's switching a drinker's preference from scotch to gin or Drambuie to Amaretto. Those are slight, perhaps even subtle changes, but when multiplied by millions and millions of Americans, add up to investment potentials.

Wines and Beef

One of the most dramatic consumptive changes of the 1970s was the strong switch in consumer preference from red wines to white wines. In my opinion, we are going to see a similar consumer preference switch take place in the '80s.

In the 1960s, when I was living in California, supposedly one of the "hottest" investment opportunities was vineyards, especially those producing the Cabernet Sauvignon grape for the production of the Cabernet Sauvignon wine. That particular red wine had really caught on. It was *the* wine to serve. In fact, people were drinking it, not only with meals, but in place of a cocktail. It was as fashionable as today's designer jeans and Perrier water.

The investment world, noticing the consumers' approval of Cabernet Sauvignon, went heavily into the development of the required vineyards. A funny thing happened along the way, however, consumers' tastes started to change and their interests shifted. The Cabernet Sauvignon grape, which still is popular and tastes as good as ever, stopped being a fad, and has now returned to being just another high quality wine—but without the snob-appeal and fashion-appeal that it had in the early to late '60s.

Instead of red-wine consumption growing and growing, American consumers, led by the new taste in cuisine, switched their preference to crisp, dry white wine; and if you know anything about wines at all, you know that Napa white wines are very very "in."

I think this change in consumer preference is going to spill over next in the meat market. Whereas the '60s and mid-'70s saw a tremendous demand by the American consumer for beef, as evidenced by the success of MacDonald's, prime rib restaurants, and steak places, I think we now have turned the corner and are going to see more and more emphasis on not red meats, but white meats, just as we went from red wines to white wines. It has already become noticeable—both MacDonald's and Burger King now sell chicken sandwiches. That's the first wide-spread sign of shift in public eating habits.

Secondly, the sales of fish have started to move; and, in fact, the majority of snob-appeal restaurants are offering very little beef on the menu. In its place they are offering a great deal of fish, or white meat dishes, such as chicken, turkey, veal, scallops, etc.

Most likely, before the end of this century, beef will be an exclusive item, eaten primarily by the wealthy. It will still be popular, but those special cuts, the Chateaubriand, New York Steak, Spencer Steak, etc. will not only cost more, but will be seen less often. They will become more of a delicacy.

There are two reasons behind this. One, the economics of beef production dictate that it takes a longer time period and more of an investment to produce a pound of beef than it does to produce, say, a pound of fish, frog legs or chicken. Also, the cost of entering the white-meat business is much lower than entering the red-meat business. More importantly, however, is the mere fact that we seem to be on the verge of a consumer change in eating habits, with the new emphasis on health, low cholesterol diets, etc. Thus, if you are involved in the food business in any way whatsoever, from production through consumption, you should be prepared for this change.

Corporation Profits and How Trends Reflect Them

Another interesting way to keep your curiosity aroused and to monitor the possibility for early trend changes, is check out those corporations that are profitable. You can do this, of course, by following the stocks of the individual companies; and if you notice that there is a group of them suddenly becoming profitable, you have more than adequate and fair warning to pay attention to this sector of the economy. A few years ago this occurred in the mobile-home industry. The few people making mobile homes started showing gargantuan profits and, sure enough, within a matter of 24 months, other people had entered what was then a new business and established a very good industry which continues to persist on a profitable basis.

Stock Relations: Collective Demand

In terms of the stock market, I suggest you think in groups, trying to see what common relationships there are between the various profitable companies. It may be that they are defense-oriented, perhaps energy-oriented, human resource-oriented; but see if there isn't some underlying current that ties them all together.

This collective demand has had an effect from time to time in the commodity market, and I think it will continue occurring. It is the demand for protein. Protein, as we all know, is one of the main sources of life. Without it life simply doesn't last very long. Thus, I have noticed during times of agricultural "crisis" that the protein items seem to move together. You may not think that there is much relationship between eggs and pork bellies, or cattle and wheat, but there is: they are protein products, and thus, act differently than, say, potatoes, orange juice, coffee, sugar and cocoa, which are also edible commodities. Commodity traders of the '80s and '90s should pay particular attention to the loosely grouped protein commodity items.

Monitoring the Media for "Fads"

Again, you should pay attention to the "fads." We are lucky, because television presents all sorts of new fads to us on a daily basis. The problem is that we are now inundated with so many things that may potentially be fads; we have to learn how to separate the wheat from the chaff. One of the better ways of doing this is to notice how much play potential fad is getting in the media. If you see the media pick it up—radio as well as television and newspapers—and you see the area's major sellers and distributors gearing up for the fad, you can rest assured that it's one that's going to be with us for some period of time.

In fact, your best broad source of information on up-and-coming trends will be the media, whether off-beat newspapers or magazines, television interviews or television shows, or new books; if you closely follow the media, I think you are going to be able to spot trends in advance.

I'm going to mention in the next few pages some of the publications that I subscribe to, to monitor what is taking place. Some of them are political, some economic, social. All have, at one time or another, helped me to forecast the appearance of consumer changes which have resulted in good investment opportunities.

Book Monitoring

Since you are reading this book, I will assume that you are an avid book reader. I hope so. You can probably get as much information about potential changes by keeping track of literature and books as just about anything I know outside of the standard media.

I would like to share with you a good case in point. Accupuncture is somewhat an off-beat area. I first read a news story on accupuncture in what was then a great magazine, True, in the early '60s. I next read a book on accupuncture in the San Francisco library in about 1963. Looking back on it, I can see there was a growing interest in America for accupuncture and other Oriental medical treatments. Yet, it wasn't until the mid-'70s that accupuncture became a profitable business venture, whether accupuncture services, writing books, doing the medical research, importing herbs from China, or whatever; this trend, which I had spotted very very early, but never participated in directly, finally arrived.

Another recent "fad" in the health area is GH3, the treatment from Romania that apparently decreases senility and, perhaps, increases longevity. There are other such treatments around, but I first came in contact with GH3 almost ten years ago, and now notice it is being advertised in some of the media. Somebody's making money off of it.

Pizza Money

Massive fortunes were made a few years ago with the mass introduction of pizza. Prior to that, we had all been interested in eating hamburgers and fried chicken; but the pizza trend spread very quickly and very profitably. You should certainly be monitoring what other changes are taking place in the American diet. One of the recent changes is that people have begun to favor alfalfa sprouts and avocado sandwiches as part of the "back to nature" health movement. Now whether you agree or disagree with the movement is immaterial. There has been money made providing services for those who choose to follow that life-style.

The Wall Street Journal

In the hard-core investment world, there is nothing that is going to provide you with more information about business and opportunity changes than *The Wall Street Journal*. Now, there are two ways to read *The Wall Street Journal*. One is the standard daily technique of reading the articles and interpreting what they are indicating. *The Wall Street Journal* staff has done a very good job of anticipating trends. Its headlines do not say, "Get Aboard the Train–It's Leaving the Station"; they just simply cover changes that are taking place within society. It's our purpose to analyze which of these trends may be profitable.

Reading the Ads

The other way to read the *Wall Street Journal* is to read its advertisements very carefully. I think that is an area that is neglected by most investors. Frankly, I am much more concerned about reading advertisements in some publications that I am in reading the editorial matter. While I may enjoy the editorial content, I am more intrigued to see what people are trying to sell me. You will continually be exposed to new ideas if you read the ads. You may not want to purchase everything you read— in fact, I suggest you don't—but you're going to see potential changes. When you notice that three or four people are getting aboard a bandwagon, it's an indication that the engine is running and the train is on its way to some destination. I also subscribe to a group of publications that I could, perhaps, best label as "counter-culture" magazines. These are the type of newspapers and magazines that you may not choose to lay on your coffee table to have your friends look at; many of them will not win friends and influence people, but their editorial staffs have done good jobs over the years of exposing people and industries that have led to changes.

Monitoring the Counter-Culture

Perhaps the very best of the more conservative counter-culture publications is the *National Spotlight*, published in Washington D.C. The *Spotlight* is a most iconoclastic weekly newspaper. Their biases are quite conservative and you probably will not agree with everything that they say editorially. But many of their advertisers have triggered major changes within the country; specifically, to my knowledge, of all the national media, Laetrile first surfaced as an advertised product in the *National Spotlight*; and the same goes for D.M.S.O. The *National Spotlight* will keep you well informed with what's happening in the government of this country, as well as other countries, and the rise and fall of gold and the dollar. I think you will also find it a very good source of information on potential governmental crises and coups throughout the globe. They've been wrong on some of their calls, but they've been spectacularly successful in calling some major political and economic changes very early on.

On the other side of the political fence, there are several publications published by Ralph Nader, such as his *Congressional Probe*. But the one far-left magazine I've enjoyed the most is *Mother Jones*. If you are in business, or even merely believe in capitalism, you're going to get your dander up every time you read *Mother Jones*. Nonetheless, its editors have uncovered some major corporate and business scandals; and those scandals have altered investment opportunities.

Perhaps the most notorious one was their attack on baby formulas. The editors contended it was safer to breast-feed babies than to feed them the formula products made by the large drug companies. Their articles alone probably began the large reversal, from Enfamil and Similac back to a more natural method of nursing children. It has been estimated that sales of Similac and Enfamil have declined almost 15% to 20%, since the *Mother Jones* articles. If you were following *Mother Jones*, you knew to get out of some rapidly depreciating investments.

There is another magazine that initially started out as an organ of the counter-culture, the *Mother Earth News*, which has become a highly respected, status quo information source. I would suggest that you subscribe, or at least monitor, the magazine, because it will not only present interesting ideas, but hits on new developments very early on. The *Mother Earth News* and the other "Earth" publications came upon several business trends very early. The trend they were most accurate about was the alternative energy craze. If you had been following those publications, you would have been well aware of the oncoming success of wood stoves, solar panels, and organic gardening. The "return to the Earth" movement was forecast loud and clear in these publications.

Prevention Is Medicinal, and Stout–Hearted "Men's"

Another publication that I have enjoyed through the years, and which also has a good record of spotting major trend changes, is *Prevention* magazine. *Prevention* is, more or less, the vitamin Bible of the business. *Prevention* was the first magazine to write seriously about the need for bran in our diet. Less than 18 months after the *Prevention* article, the "brand band" was drummed up, and bran and fiber was added to everything in our diet, from cereal to bread. The readers of *Prevention* knew this trend was coming.

Some of the major political changes and fast-rising political personalities have also gotten good press early on in the men's magazines. *True*, for example, documented the Cuban Revolution months before it took place. By "men's magazines," I'm not referring to the pornographic variety, although, from time to time, there have been superb articles that have either brought about, or heralded, change in both *Penthouse* and *Playboy*. *Penthouse* seems to take a more aggressive editorial stance and has published some tremendous articles that have, and are, bringing about change, in cancer cures, governmental regulations, etc. Even one that recently appeared in *Penthouse*, saying that sex education in schools was a negative, not a positive. I'm certain the tone of that article surprised *Penthouse* readers as much as its appearance in *Penthouse* surprised those who are opposed to sex education in public schools.

I would also suggest that you become a card-carrying member of the National Taxpayers' Union, if you are politically concerned. The National Taxpayers' Union is a coalition of people throughout the country who are extremely concerned that we have a balanced budget and less government. They are one of the driving forces behind this over-all trend, are non-partisan, and do an effective job of helping to get people elected, as well as legislation passed through both houses of Congress and Senate.

Assorted Monitors

Other magazines that I do not subscribe to, but do monitor from time to time and will pick up on the newsstand, include *Variety*, for the entertainment business, and *Esquire*, which, in my opinion, has gone downhill recently, but in the past has been able to anticipate some economic changes. There have been several new magazines that I have gotten a good deal of information out of, such as *Omni*, *Discover*, *Energy Medicine*, and *Executive Intelligence Review*. There has also been some good background information in *Forbes* and *Business Week* from time to time.

Remember, investment opportunities do not always appear on the business pages of newspapers. Frequently, and most of the very best ones, occur on the front pages. The *New York Times* has, perhaps, the very best and widest editorial coverage that's ever been provided by a daily newspaper. It has correspondents throughout the globe; as does the *Los Angeles Times*. These publications are invaluable if you read them and consider how the news content will affect matters, and then ask yourself if the resulting change is going to mean a good investment opportunity. Don't neglect reading their business opportunity sections in the classifieds. You'll learn more about new trends and businesses there than in a year of grad school.

The trick to spotting a change—a new trend—is to remember

that virtually every single problem that has ever presented it-self to mankind has actually been an opportunity. People don't like to have problems. People like to either avoid problems or get them solved. People like to have problems eliminated from their lives, and, for the most part, are willing to pay for the elimination of those problems, whether it's a health problem, an economic problem, or simply a matter of drawers not rolling out smoothly from their desks. Those little inconveniences can amount to some nice investment opportunities.

Yale Hirsch's Smart Money

One individual who has a very good record of spotting trends early is my good friend, Yale Hirsch, who publishes *Smart Money*. Yale is not only an extremely intelligent and capable fellow; he also, like myself, is optimistic about the future of the country. For that reason, instead of delving in gold and diamonds, Yale is more concerned with where we are going as a country and how we're solving the problems of the country. Yale has monitored, on an investment basis, perhaps better than anyone else, the changes in the energy industry, biogenetics, etc. A subscription to Yale's publication would probably be a must for any stock trader who is looking to get aboard early trains.

What You Should, and Should Not, Buy at the Grocery Store

Believe it or not, you'll also get some good information, from time to time, from the grocery weeklies, like the *National Enquirer*. Several articles have appeared in the *National Enquirer* that later appeared in *Time, Newsweek,* and even the *New York Times,* that have triggered trends.

Incidentally, as far as I'm concerned, by the time something appears in the news weeklies the trend has probably already begun, and is upon its way. To use my analogy, the train is way out of the station, and, in fact, you probably can't even see the caboose!

When to Board the Train

Well, there it is! I've given you some of my best investment sources. You probably have some of your own. I'm also supplying you with a list of other newspapers and magazines that I try to either browse through, or read on an irregular basis, because I've noticed they also have an ability to write about information that later on gains some popularity. What I hope you'll remember is that it is more profitable to get aboard a train early than late; and even getting aboard a train late is better than not getting aboard a train at all.

I would not jump aboard any fad or potential trend on a willy-nilly basis. It must be something you understand and enjoy. I think you need to do some homework and do your own thinking, to see if, in fact, it's going to be popular in the long term, to figure out what sort of impact it will have on the economy. Once you see these things developing, it becomes much easier to select your investment vehicles, whether in the stock market or not. Perhaps Carly Simon's song, "Anticipation", should be the theme song of everyone seeking investment changes.

The Race

Historically speaking, mankind has never just stagnated for more than seven years. We are probably leaving one of those stagnating periods right now, which means the rate of change, economically and sociologically, is going to be beyond most of our expectations over the next twenty years.

The pace of life is speeding up! The rate at which things change, whether it's how fast we go or how long we live, is going to be different. Consider a report by the world-famous demographer, George Myers, of Duke University, which says that the chances of anyone dying between the ages of fifty to fifty-five have dropped by almost 25% in the last twenty-five years. For people between the ages of fifty-five to sixty there has been a 23% drop in the chances of dying; those between the ages of sixty to sixty-five have experienced a 20% decline; as have those in the seventy-five to eight-five bracket. This, then, will be the major change in the shape of things to come.

We're simply going to have people living longer than we've ever thought possible. The implications of this are staggering. How long people will be working, what social security payments will be, how much recreation time will there be for people, what sort of new family relationships will develop: all these, and more, are new issues that have been raised by the decrease in the death rate. The increase in population boils down to one simple fact: there will be an increase in investment opportunities, because all those people will persevere and survive, and will have more needs and desires. They'll also have more money to pay for those needs and desires.

So—At Last—Is the Apocalypse at Hand?
A Scenario

While private entrepreneurs abound telling us that the apocalypse is about to hit, so far the only public announcement of this kind I know has come from Lester Goddard, Nevada's Savings and Loan Commissioner. He has gone public with his warning that all the planets in the solar system are going to team up in a perfect line, which he calls a "deadly row," creating earthquakes and tidal waves throughout the globe. He has said, "The spectacular changes may not take place for the next twelve months or so. During this dark cycle of the Earth I am again going to warn about impending financial collapse in 1982 and 1983, with a resultant depression and collapse of the real estate market leading to World War III by the end of the decade." Mr. Goddard, I think, points to a major problem, from time to time, I ask myself: "Exactly what is my stop/loss protection in the event I'm wrong in my optimism for the '80s and '90s? What's my protection?"

I think protection can come in a variety of ways. First of all, if the great earthquake hits California and it, Nevada, Utah, and Colorado slide into the ocean, I don't think there's much that any of us can really do to protect ourselves, other than to be far away when it happens. But that is simply an impossibility. Everyone cannot move out of New York City or Los Angeles and come to Montana or parts of Canada that supposedly are safe from the projected cataclysmic events.

I mean after all, life does have its ups and downs, and if we do get the apocalypse that's been forecast, it happens. The fact that you have dehydrated food and your basement full of gold is not going to make any difference if the state you're living in slips into the ocean. For that matter, it's probably not going to make much difference how much gold or diamonds you own if we have a major war. You may be able to buy yourself out of some problems for awhile, but eventually someone is going to find out about your gold and they're going to come with bigger guns than you have, and you're going to end up sacrificing your gold in exchange for your life.

Frankly, I don't find gold nearly as valuable as a good breathing apparatus, after having lived through the disruption of Mount Saint Helens; we are approximately four hundred and fifty miles away from the volcano. I have learned that there is nothing more precious to us than air. You can have dehydrated food and bars of silver. I'll take a mask that allows me to breathe any time!

Can you imagine in the event of a nuclear disaster, whether it's through the eruption of a nuclear energy facility or a war, just how long you're going to last if you can't breathe? We certainly learned it in the Flathead Valley. I always chuckle because one of the leading forecasters of doom-and-gloom chose to live in my part of Montana. He announced to his following that it was a safe area, protected by the wind currents from the possibility of nuclear fallout.What a joke! Though we were so far away from Mount Saint Helens, we literally could not see more than two blocks ahead for days on end. Stores and businesses were closed by state law. We had to wear masks, couldn't go outside of our homes, and couldn't even drive our cars out of the disaster, because our engines plugged up with the fine volcanic ash.

If you're "into" survival, then my first comment to you would be to make certain that you do have breathing apparatus. Secondly, you're going to need water, which you can store by having it canned, or choosing to live in an area remote enough where you can have a well that will not be polluted.

The third item that you are going to need, of course, will be food. There has been a big rage to move to dehydrated food.

One author may have summed it up best when he said he'd "Rather take his chance with rioters than eating that dehydrated stuff!" Some of the "dehydrated stuff" is probably much worse than facing rioters and looters, but it has improved substantially in quality over the recent years, and the possibilities of its going stale have been pretty much eliminated by the magic of the "freeze-dried" process.

If you are interested in buying freeze-dried food as a stop-gap protection, then I would suggest you contact Mountain Home, in Albany, Oregon. They seem to have the best products.

One of the problems with freeze-dried food, though, is that a few months supply of freeze-dried food is not going to fit into your car. It takes up a substantial amount of space. You're either going to have to have it buried at a pre-determined site or have to have a caravan deliver it for you to your hideaway.

There is a possibility that you may be able to prolong life on Earth for a good period of time without freeze-dried food. The substance I'm going to suggest you buy is not particularly palatable, even compared to freeze-dried foods; it lacks flavor and texture and all of the other things that makes eating one of the finer enjoyments of life. But it will keep you alive, it's very storable, and you can maintain a six months supply of most all of the nourishment that you're going to need in the trunk of your car and still have *room left over!*

What I'm talking about is an algae that has been developed in Japan. I'm referring to Spiralina algae. The best thing about Spiralina is that it is extremely high in protein, with five assimilable grams per tablespoon. That's very good when you consider that you need anywhere from 25 to 65 grams of protein a day, depending on your body type. About the only thing that Spiralina does not adequately provide is vitamin B-12, which, of course, you would be able to take in vitamin supplements, available at your local drug or health food store.

There are many recorded instances of people fasting for over sixty days on a diet of nothing but some juices and Spiralina. I sure don't claim miracles for Spiralina, but if you are curious about how you can possibly prolong yourself during disaster, this looks to me like the easiest way to provide yourself at a very low cost, with a life-sustaining diet. I imagine you can buy a six month's supply of Spiralina for less than $100 per person; whereas, the same amount of freeze-dried food is going to cost you about one thousand dollars.

The Energy Picture in the Years to Come

As I mentioned earlier, the big energy move over the next twenty years should be away from hydro-carbon fuels. We should continue with nuclear fission, and solar will also be brought into use, as developing technology allows us to install solar heating into our homes. But the major industrial energy sources will not be solar; solar energy is not yet that far along, and may never be. So, as I see it, nuclear fusion is simply the password to the energy requirements of the next century. Anything that involves nuclear fusion is going to prosper.

I suspect you're going to see nuclear fusion energy generation occur in a variety of ways. There will be very large plants, as well as tiny fusion facilities, where you plug in the nuclear power source. When your nuclear "battery" runs down, you just take it out and plug in another one.

But there is money to be made in solar; and, toward the end of the decade, there will be big money in hydro-carbon, especially coal, oil and shale. However, the long-term environmental implications of hydro-carbon energy conversion is troubling. We will be able to get energy in the future, but we must not do it at the cost of destroying our environment.

A basic law of physics says that energy cannot be destroyed, and it can't. The energy is there. But the environment *can* be destroyed on a permanent basis and never brought back to its present beauty.

Unwinding Along the Highways

Recently, engineers at UCLA announced that they have come up with a snappy new way to propel cars. Dr. Andrew Charwat has been working on devising a way of capturing the energy that is lost by a car as it brakes to a stop.

What takes place currently when a car brakes to a stop is that energy is lost, in that the forward momentum the car has is dissipated by the braking action of the car. Dr. Charwat has been working on a method that will capture that energy by rechanneling it into gigantic rubber bands in the car where it could be stored. Charwat says that such a device would be a simple configuration, with eighteen to twenty rubber bands stretched around a hydrolic piston. The energy lost in braking would be re-captured. A hydrolic pump motor, mounted on the wheels, would generate pressure during braking. The reverse would happen when the energy was used to accelerate the vehicle.

Gas Prices

One scenario possibility in the energy crisis first raised its ugly head in the summer of 1981. What's taken place is that, for the first time, we've started to see down ticks in the price of gas at the gasoline stations. Not much—a penny here, a penny there—but it does appear that the price of gasoline has either stabilized or has stopped heading downward. Here's a scenario: the OPEC nations now realize that the decontrol of energy prices in America has led to more discovery and more production and so they decide to lower their prices substantially. Let's say they stabilize oil to the point where gasoline costs $.95 to $1.00 a gallon. That would effectively break all the people who recently invested heavily in programs, such as the Northern Tier Pipeline, across the state of Montana, or the North Sea Project, which has been so beneficial to England. In short, if the OPEC nations want to really play hard ball, they would lower the price substantially. Thus, the projects that have come on-stream recently would be shut down, because they could not deliver hydro-carbons at the same low rate as OPEC. Thus, we would get back into our OPEC addiction, shut down our capital investments, and scare off anyone else from coming into the capitalization required to bring these projects on-stream at a later date.

At that later date, once OPEC has broken down everyone's opportunity to develop the market, OPEC then starts raising the price back up, in one swift, quick move to, say, $1.50 or

$2.00 a gallon. At that point they have broken their competition through an effective price war, and can then take the cost of gasoline to wherever they like.

This is not a particularly pleasurable scenario, and one that I hope doesn't develop, but it is certainly one that the astute investor, and energy user, should be on top of.

The War on Cancer

The biggest health battle—and it's one I predict we are going to win by the end of the decade—is the one against cancer. The medical profession seems to have a firm commitment to coming up with workable cures for cancer. In addition to that, there are additional therapies also being offered that seem to be having an affect on curing or stopping the growth of a cancer. Consider, if you will, just some of the following medical developments; Dr. James Harrell, clinical professor of medicine at the University of California Medical Center in La Jolla, has developed a flexible "Broncho-scope," basically a cable that is fed through a patient's lung. It has a radiation needle that can go directly into the tumors in the bronchial passage areas. Prior to this, it was impossible to perform radiation therapy on the bronchial passage areas. Now with the cable it can be done. The cable has light-carrying fibers that enable a physician to see the tumor itself. With the needle threaded directly under the tumor, radioactive seeds, about an inch long, and as thick as a pencil lead, are planted with the tip of the needle.

Doctor Theodore Phillips, at the University of California at San Francisco, has developed a treatment using Misonidazole to make radiation therapy work more effectively. One of the problems now, according to Doctor Phillips, is that as a tumor develops, it loses oxygen, which makes it much more resistant to radiation. However, the addition of Misonidazole breaks down this defense by oxygenating the cancer cell, so the radiation can bombard through.

Pancreas and Diabetes

Not quite as esoteric, and easier to understand, comes a development from the University of Minnesota Medical School, where Doctor Henry Buchwald has just implanted the world's first artificial pancreas. The device is obviously not a true pancreas, but is, rather, a small pump, which acts like a pancreas to produce a steady trickle of insulin into the blood stream.

Recent government statistics show that there are probably ten million Americans with diabetes, and almost two million of them need daily insulin injections. I don't mean to sound crass and cruel, but that means there is a market of well over two million people who are potential purchasers of the artificial pancreas, should the idea prove itself in actual practice.

Alternative Medicine: Vitamin Cures

My own personal orientation tells me that some of the more tremendous strides forward will be made through non-traditional approaches, with vitamins and vitamin therapy leading the way.

I've had involvement with alternative healing processes. Some of these are absolutely mind-boggling, such as watching the works of the psychic healers in the Phillippines, which I still have many questions about. But I'm not nearly as skeptical about what the effect of vitamins and minerals has been on me as well as on other people I've seen use them.

Just recently, one of the world's largest drug manufacturers, Hoffman-LaRoche, a Swiss based drug firm, issued a report saying that vitamin B-3, Niacin (or Niacinamide) produces, essentially, the same results in people as Librium or Valium. Now, the news isn't that they both produce the same results; The news is that vitamin B-3 is as safe, taken in even large quantities, as drinking water. Doctor John Beaton, a Ph.D. at the University of Alabama, has said of vitamin B-3: "It is a sedative, and there is no question that it demonstrates anti-aggression, anti-anxiety and anti-convulsion effects. It has valium-like effects. It certainly improves the quality of human sleep." I ask you: which will sell the best—Valium, with its bad name and side effects, or the vitamin?

Another study, conducted in England, shows that people who take large doses of vitamin A regularly are much less susceptible to getting cancer than people of similar backgrounds and habits, even among smokers.

I think this is going to be the most spectacular, and certainly the most personally rewarding, area for us to focus our attention on in the coming years. You may enjoy Lawrence Lamb's book, *Get Ready for Immortality* (Harper and Row). Doctor Lamb's thesis is that we are on the verge of a breakthrough that will bring people very close to the immortality that man has searched for throughout the millenia.

He thoroughly discusses the effects of longevity drugs and treatments ranging from DNA to self-therapy for rejuvenation, and even Gerovital GH-3. One of the main causes of aging is oxydization within the body, and oxydization can be stopped by proper vitamin intake, specifically, vitamins A, C and E, which are well known and well documented in all medical literature as being anti-oxydants.

I don't know if I agree with Doctor Lamb that immortality will soon be upon us, but I *am* clearly convinced that there are those among mankind who are going to live an enjoyable, livable life well beyond one hundred years.

Migraines

We may even see gargantuan breakthroughs in health items as mundane as the commonplace migraine headache that supposedly affects twelve to sixteen million Americans every week, who suffer such agonizing head pains that they simply can't perform and, in many cases, can't even go to work.

Dr. Alan Levin, an Associate Professor of Dermatology at the University of Southern California, School of Medicine, Dr. Miller, a pioneering allergist in private practice in Mobile, Alabama, and other doctors, have concluded that most migraines are due to food allergies. The problem, of course, is detecting which food is causing the allergy that creates the migraine. In the past, the medical profession has attempted to stop migraines through painkillers. Those painkillers were sold and created fortunes for the sellers. The new medical approach, however, is to use weak injections of the same food substance that causes the migraine incident. This is similar to injecting a virus to build up the body's tolerance of a larger dose of the virus. Dr. Levin has suggested that the majority of migraines could be cured by taking such injections twice a week for a good number of weeks, and then, after that, phasing into a longer-term, perhaps monthly, program. Whether you've ever had a migraine, or whether the only migraine you've ever had has come from not having profitable investments, or passing by investment opportunities that later turned out to be spectacular, this just points out again the revolutionary changes we are going to see in medicine, and how the astute investor who knows those companies developing a new way of treating people can profit.

Gerontology

Certainly, the most interesting and profitable work that is going to be done outside of the bio-genetic engineering will be in the area of Gerontology. I hope you'll listen closely to just what some doctors in the Gerontology area have said recently. Dr. Alvin Silverstein, Professor of Biology at the City University of New York's College of Staten Island has said that breakthroughs over the next ten to fifteen years could reward us with an incredibly long lifespan, and, if advances continue as they have in recent years, you will live to be over 100 years old if you are alive in the 1990s.

Dr. Paul Segall, a PhD in Gerontology and a life extension specialist, has said that it is no longer pie-in-the-sky to talk of living 150 years or more.

Dr. Ronald Harper, Director of the Gerontology Center at the University of Kansas, declares that by the end of the 1990s, "Man could have an average life expectancy well beyond 100 years."

There are two questions to ask? First, how in the heck are they going to do it? And secondly, what investment and social changes will this bring about?

These and other doctors and scientists have already begun studying genes that control aging, and are seeking ways to manipulate them for a longer life. They have discovered some amazing youth hormones that not only slow down aging in animals, but, to some extent, reverse the aging process. Obviously, they are not going to take an 80-year-old man and make him a 20-year-old kid; but all the same they *can* reverse the aging process in animals to some degree.

We've already seen the success with artificial organs. Some researchers even claim that it may be possible to regrow, at least partially, organs that are wearing out. Gene manipulation, in one form or another, may mean that the average person theoretically could live for hundreds of years; Dr. Julian Whitaker, Director of the California Heart Medical Clinic, in Huntington Beach, California, has said as much.

If you think the possibility for regeneration is a bit too far out, consider that fingertips that have been cut off of children have sometimes grown back, as have partially removed spleens and even livers. Researchers are now busy trying to determine exactly what causes a regeneration. One group of these scientists believes that regeneration is triggered by the secretion of a substance from nerve endings. In theory, if this is correct, and scientists can pinpoint the mechanism that causes this secretion, we will have opened the door to regeneration.

While the majority of the things in the above paragraphs seem a little far out, remember that a heart transplant seemed totally impossible twenty years ago.

Economic Changes

I have already dealt at length with some of the economic changes that are going to take place in the coming years; but I want to drive home one more time the importance of tax cuts, and what their economic impact has been.

In recent history we have had three major tax cuts. The first occurred in 1964 when the Dow Jones Industrial Average stood at 750. One year later the Dow Jones Industrial Average stood at 899 for a 20% gain. Then, in February of 1975, we had a substantial tax rebate. At that time the Dow was standing at 647. One year later it was at 958, for a 58% gain. Finally, we had a tax reduction on January 1, 1976 and the Dow was at 784. One year later the Dow stood at 1,004, for a 28% gain. I think this is pretty conclusive evidence that tax cuts stimulate the market. If you take the price level of the stock market when

Ronald Reagan won the election—937—and add the minimum gain of the last three tax cuts, 20%, you see that the Dow should move at least into the 1,000 area in the first year or two.

You may want to compare and make your own projection. You may want to take the price of the Dow Jones Industrial Average when the Reagan tax cuts go into effect, and add, at least 20% to that figure. That would be another outside target for the movement of the market.

If you are not exposed to the world of high finance on a daily basis, you don't really know what's going on around us all the time; so I would like to show you just some of what other people are doing for the future.

Westinghouse

Let's take a company you are probably familiar with, Westinghouse Electric. They have decided that over the next five years, just to expand and modernize their electronic center in Baltimore, they will spend over $100 million. They are spending $31 million for three new research facilities and $8 million to increase productivity of computer aids. Obviously, Westinghouse Electric is not listening to the doomsday crowd.

The Import–Export Bank

The United States Import-Export Bank recently approved loans adding up to $46½ million; these are direct loans to borrowers in Mexico, Japan and Algeria for the purchase of United States materials. Obviously, the members of the United States Import-Export Bank are not listening to the doom-and-gloomers either.

To show you just how complex and intriguing all this has become, I'd like to call your attention to Sord Computer Systems in Japan. Sord markets computers throughout the world. While they are a Japanese company based in Tokyo, they are just now opening up a plant, at a cost of $6 million, in, of all places, Ireland!

People with money, major corporations, are not digging in to the trenches. They're planning to move forward.

At Home in New York With The Doom-and-Gloomers

While the doom-and-gloom crowd has been predicting that the real-estate market is going to fall apart, recent reports out of New York show that properties in downtown Manhattan (supposedly the worst of the worse places to invest in real estate) have increased 124% in the four years starting with 1975. That's a gain comensurate with gold. Actually, when one considers the tax implications one gets from investing in real estate versus investing in gold, downtown New York City property values were a better investment vehicle than gold. Perhaps that's why Gerald Hines, a Houston real estate developer, recently paid a record $28 million, for a small chunk of a block in downtown Manhattan that represents less than one third of the block. Hines shelled out $1,000 per square foot.

Most interesting is that Hines purchased the real estate from Citibank, which bought the lot only last year for seven million dollars. Citibank was going to put up a residential building, but decided against it. Yet, in the midst of what is supposedly a depression, when a bank doesn't want to develop the property, Mr. Hines had no trouble coming up with the money to carry out the concept of developing downtown Manhattan!

Play It Again (and Again), Sam

As I mentioned earlier, the most lucrative investment area *is* entertainment. We're going to have more leisure time, and more of us are becoming more bored with television, so there will need to be other entertainment vehicles; whether it's outdoor recreation, return to the theater, another type of television . . . it doesn't matter. It's your job to keep your eyes peeled on these entertainment developments.

Hopefully, I can drive home to you the importance of paying attention to what's happening in the entertainment world by relating to you the story of *La Cage Aux Folles*. This is a French motion picture, which was initially released in a little New York City theater. The plot of the movie doesn't sound like it would ever go any place at all: it is the story of the trials and tribulations of the owner of a homosexual bar in San Tropez, and his boy-friend, the bar's main attraction: he is a drag queen. Even the initial reviews of the movie were not too friendly. But for some ungodly reason, it caught on with the New York crowd. The movie grossed over $4 million in its 83 week run in The Big Apple. During its final week, the movie grossed almost ten thousand dollars. Frankly, I don't go much for homosexual movies; but it certainly is a strong indication of changing tastes in entertainment, as well as the investment opportunity the entertainment field can provide.

We can't all own our own football franchise, but the mania we have seen in football followers, whether it's the Oakland Raiders (Los Angeles Raiders?), San Diego Chargers, the Denver Broncos or Dallas Cowboys, proves that it would be extremely profitable for someone to make a public offering to put together a football or basketball team. In a major metropolitan area it would be easy to raise the money. The people are there; and they want to have their hometown teams they can be proud of. I think the growth of professional sports leagues will represent an unparalled investment opportunity in the next fifteen to twenty years. At some time we'll most likely get a little tired of Monday night football, and then we will see new types of team-sport concepts evolve.

I believe that will take place, because people like the unity concept. We have not had a good deal of unity in America recently. But sports fans have. They can find that unity with whatever team sport they decide to support. Additionally, more people want to get out more of the time now, instead of just watching television and reading. They want to actively enjoy all entertainment, which accounts for the tremendous increase in the success of "dude" ranches, ski resorts, and the like. Watch for that trend to continue.

It's Hard to Trust Anyone in the Investment Advisory Business

One thing that will stay the same in the world of finance is that a good number of the supposed experts will continue being wrong the majority of the time. Henry Kauffman, a partner of Solomon Brothers, one of the world's most exclusive investment banking firms, wrote an article for the *Wall Street Journal* in which he forecasted higher interest rates. Two days after his forecast, interest rates began to decline by almost two-and-one-half percentage points.

This is not an anomaly. The same thing happened in the spring of 1980, when he forecast that rates would go quite a bit higher, and, again in two days, rates began to decline almost ten percentage points. The same forecast was also made by several leading brokerage firms at the same time. This just proves the old adage, "It's hard to trust anyone in the investment advisory business." They are not trying to mislead you; it's just that so many people have so many different ideas of what is going to take place.

Fun and Profit

Next, I'd like to turn your attention to some of the fun things that should be happening as the twentieth century draws itself to a close. One of the most exciting was reported recently in the December 1980 issue of *Science News* under the headline: "Ticker Tape Bacteria."

It seems scientists have been able to direct one type of micro-organism to produce long, fibrous ribbons of cellulose. This is one of the first examples of genetic engineering, and has immediate application to the investment world.

Malcolm Brown, of the University of North Carolina in Chapel Hill, is working on bacteria using inexpensive chemicals to spin a fiber-like material that could be used as thread. The "bug" spins twisted ribbons of pure cellulose through a sequential clustering process. Each of the bacteria produce three to four millimeters of cellulose ribbon each day. The next issue will be whether the micro-organisms can produce fiber rapidly enough for commercial use. At this time it appears there is a good chance that the clothes of the later part of this decade will come literally from an unlimited source of bacteria that will spin away night and day to produce thread for mankind.

You must pay close attention to this whole area of genetics. After all, the first genetic stock to go public, Genetech, quickly went from thirty-five to eighty-nine dollars a share. It has pulled back a bit since then. Obviously, informed money can appreciate the potential for genetic research and developments.

Bio-Feedback

Along with genetic research, I'm certain we're going to see more work done on bio-feedback. Most likely, some bright entrepreneur is going to establish a franchise of bio-feedback centers, just as we have diet centers franchised throughout the country.

A great many physical ailments can be taken care of with the bio-feedback techniques, ranging all the way from the pain of migraine headaches to motion-sickness. Bio-feedback works by attaching electrodes to vital nerve centers, thus enabling a person to monitor his physiological reactions to various things. As such, you can learn to control body functions and eliminate pain.

Reviewing the Future

Let's just quickly review some of the possibilities that may change things quite a bit in the next twenty years. These are not just ivory-tower changes, but changes that people are working on now and are close to bringing about. I have told you about Spiralina; you must also realize that other work is being done along this line to provide relief for people in famine or disaster-struck areas of the globe. People will still feel hunger pains, but they will be given a tablet, or powder, or something very much like Spiralina that would prevent starvation from occurring.

We've also gone to the other extreme and are working on creating non-food food. These are items that the body cannot use or absorb and convert to fat. Such products, in theory, would be an ideal way for someone to diet. You would be able to eat as many of these non-food items as possible, but not gain weight. Most likely, the items could be colored and flavored to be relatively palatable. We already have the technology to take proteins from bacteria and synthesize them with yeast to produce foods that are not too bad. In fact, we already have artificial steaks, which do look and, to some extent taste, like the real thing.

Jules Verne's writings discuss the possibility of mining the ocean floor. Now we have ships ready to dredge the bottom of the ocean in search of precious and usable metals. At the same time, the ships may be hauling down icebergs to areas low on water. Some entrepreneurial government or industry will most likely start mining the moon some time within the next thirty years. One of the most immediate changes we will see take place will be that of air transportation.

Some of the research being done in air transportation now centers on methods of saving energy. The industry has already begun, but we should see reductions of energy usage almost to a 30% level within the next fifteen years. Certainly planes will not be as heavily staffed as they are now. Already, some planes are run almost exclusively on automatic pilot control.

The idea that I like best is already in operation; planes with beds rather than just chairs. Obviously, for short flights, it doesn't mean much, but it sure does on trans-continental flights.

Antiques

Another investment opportunity rests in the collection of rare items, whether stamps, old cars or antiques. There certainly will be money made in this investment vehicle. I've not discussed it in this book to any extent, simply because it is a very sophisticated investment technique. One must be on guard every single moment of every single transaction to make certain he is not being had by someone selling him something that really doesn't have the value he claims for it. If you are interested in these types of investments, fine, but you're going to have to do a great deal of research to make certain you are a specialist in the area; hence, you have to know exactly what you are getting into.

War

In the event that we go to war in the next coming twenty years (which I do not think will happen), it will be played by different rules and in different ways. One of the more unusual techniques of war being developed is by the French, who have been working with neutrons to develop a neutron bomb since the 1970s. Most likely, they will be ready to go into operation with it about 1983. They are also working on plans for building a neutron barrier across their eastern frontier. This, basically, would amount to a nuclear-fortified zone about 1,000 kilometers long and 20 kilometers wide. It consists of a group of small neutron bombs, which would be triggered in the event of an attack, producing an unbroken belt of radiation that would be deadly to any living being. There is no way you could go through the belt without dying, even if you were encased in heavy armour. This would certainly be a way of keeping an aggressive nation outside of France's, or any other country's, boundaries.

Computer Education and Government Size

Many changes will take place in education in the next few years, but perhaps the most noteworthy one will come from the computer generation. Most likely, by the end of the century, there will be two types of people: those who can program computers and those who can't. The advent of small, home-size computers makes it almost mandatory for more students to become familiar with basic FORTRAN and COBOL. It has been estimated that almost 80% of American homes will have computers by 1990. They will be used for school assignments; doing office work at home; family budget; and, of course, game playing.

Hopefully, the size of the government will have diminished within the next fifteen years, but we must still be on guard for an increase in government and the changes such an increase will cause in the investment community. There may well be a trend toward more "democracy" to the United States, but we should remember that "pure democracy" really amounts to mob-ocracy. Hopefully, our citizenry will remember that we were intended to be a democratic republic. Many people have concluded that one of the causes of wars, which are wasteful and destructive, is to make profits for the super mega-bankers of the world, and stabilize governments to improve the value of paper money. If there is any validity to that in theory, and if we do go back to the gold standard, the implication would be that it would be very difficult, or non-purposeful for the mega-bankers, if such a power structure truly does exist, to bring about a war. If paper money does tend to produce war, then hard currency should produce peace.

A New Republican Era?

Assuming President Ronald Reagan will serve out two terms in office, which I hope will be the case, one might well ask, "How will the power of the Presidency be transferred? Will it go to a Democrat, or a Republican, and in what fashion? In whose hands will the power ultimately rest?"

A good deal of professional survey work has been done in this area. Combine that with a bit of political guesswork, and some pretty interesting possibilities arise.

The Republican Party has the opportunity, in fact its last opportunity, not only to turn the economics of the country around, but once again to make it fashionable to be a Republican. The majority of surveys now show that there has been a definite change: more people are saying they tend to vote Republican or tend to affiliate with the Republican Party than we have seen in the last twenty, or even thirty, years.

If, in fact, President Ronald Reagan's economic program works, as I suspect it will based not only on the program itself but on the cyclical implications of what's happening now, this is the time when our economy should be on the upbeat, and that alone will account for a good deal of improvement.

That improvement will be seen by the people as a reflection of Republican politics. Right or wrong, the Republican Party will get credit for the pickup in the economy, for the improvement of people's life-styles, for the lessening of inflation, and for lower interest rates. If the combination of supply-side economics and less government works and economic tides do rise for people in the country, the Republican Party is simply going to be *the* Party for at least the next three generations. It will take at least that long before politicians either revert back to the old spendthrift ways, or simply blow the lead they'll have.

The other side of the coin, of course, is that if the Reagan Administration policies do not work, you can simply kiss the Republican Party good-bye, as the public perception will be something to the effect of, "Gee, we gave them their shot at it, and their ideas and theories didn't work. We'll never try that again."

New Stars On the Horizon

Assuming things do work out for the good of the country, the question remains, who will be the next leader in the Republican Party?

Ronald Reagan, is, on an almost daily basis, becoming a legend in his time and one of the greatest of America's presidents. He will continue to be the "Father Figure" of the Party. In fact, it is interesting: at a time when the majority of us have been looking for some young, dynamic Whiz Kid to turn this country on again, the leadership comes from the oldest President this country has ever seen. That alone should tell you how remarkable the man, Ronald Reagan, really is.

It would be most obvious to say that Vice-President George Bush would take over the controls of the Republican Party, following the end of Reagan's term in office. However, if I were a betting man on matters of this nature, I think I would definitely lay my wager on Republican Congressman Jack Kemp.

Kemp lacks the organizational abilities that Bush has, and, in a way, seems almost lackadaisical about organizing beyond his own constituents. Nonetheless, Jack Kemp is *the* Rising Star in the Republican community, and is the person you should follow the closest as the next potential President of the United States of America.

There are two reasons for this. First, Vice-President Bush does not have the strong following of the conservative element of the Republican Party that is going to be necessary to win the primaries. Jack Kemp, on the other hand, has the conservative qualifications that are looked for and should draw a good deal of Libertarian support as well. In addition, Kemp is the most charismatic national politician we have seen since President John Kennedy. This is not to say that he is more charismatic than Reagan. Reagan's strength is not the excitement of his personality, but the excitement of his ideas, and his ability to get the job done. Jack Kemp is definitely an exciting, charismatic person; the type of guy who walks into a room and heads turn. He is an impeccable speaker, and, in addition to being articulate, is intelligent, a rare quality for a politician. So, when it comes to doing your political planning, if you are a Republican, I would plan on doing it with Jack Kemp.

In the Democratic Corner We Have . . .

It's a bit more difficult to analyze what's going to happen in the Democratic Party over the coming years. Assume they will just struggle along, because of the resurgence of Republicanism. The players in the game look like this:

First of all, Ted Kennedy's political future is behind him. He will most likely stay a Senator as long as he lives in Massachusetts, but his ability to get elected to higher office is a thing of the past.

There exists the possibility that former Vice President, Walter Mondale, will pull together the Democratic Party and move it forward to the point that he becomes the "Golden One." However, from my own contacts with the former vice president, I doubt if he has what it takes, in terms of public appeal, as well as his politics, to carry the broad support of this great country.

There are a few other possible national leaders within the Democratic Party: Senator Proxmire, perhaps, who is probably better known than any other Democratic leader, and has a higher voter approval rating. Of course, Jerry Brown will be in there too; but seems to be stuck with a similar image to George Bush's. Neither comes off as a heavyweight.

One of the reasons the Democratic Party will most likely continue on the decline is it does not, on a national level, have a stable of potential presidential candidates that can capture the excitement of this country. The big thing to be watching for in Democratic politics, then, is the emergence of this type of a candidate. The Democrats need to come up with an answer to

Ronald Reagan, Jack Kemp, George Bush. If they can do that, then I suggest you follow that person closely. If you are a Democrat, those are the coattails you are going to want to attach yourself to. At this time, there simply is not a strong, dominant figure in the Democratic Party. Until one does come along, nationally, the Democratic Party is going to founder back and forth, yet, on a local level, experience some stunning victories.

Hi-Tech

The next twenty to fifty years should provide some of the most interesting and exciting years of the annals of recorded history. The first part of the 1980s should be the initial buffer into the transition zone of space-age high technology.

Then, as we move into the next century, high technology will become king. At one time brute strength was king, then thinking was king, then the machine-age became king, and then technology became king. We are now entering into high technology, as our information and data based on the way things work has been dramatically improved. The big salaries of the coming years will not go to the doctors and lawyers, as in the past, but to the well-trained technician. Being one who is not, by nature, a technician, I find that a little sad, but also feel it is, hopefully, beneficial, because as we do become a more technical society, I think we're going to see a new combination of creativity and technique.

Conclusion: Boundless Opportunity

If you take time to stop and think about your business, profession, or occupation for just a few moments, you're bound to realize there are some tremendous opportunities for change to improve the type of work you do over the next fifteen or twenty years. The intelligent person will not only think about the change, but will come up with the ideas for the direction of change and profit from many of these ideas.

And there will be so many changes in behavior patterns of

consumers regarding what consumers want, that if you just keep your ear tuned and go with the flow, you will have opportunity after opportunity presented to you on gold and silver platters.

Despite what you may have heard from others, our great United States of America does have a future, and it is one absolutely incredible future; an outrageously positive future, which is nice for the investor, as it presents numerous investment opportunities for us, and nice for history, too.

Though we are entering a new age economically, we must remember that the same old basic economic rules of the universe prevail; they're just like physical laws and the rule of gravity, and they will maintain themselves, because, after all, there are no "free lunches" in the world, and each individual must take total responsibility. There are no instant passes to Nirvana; quality items will always be appreciated more than non-quality items.

An improvement in the quality of life in America will be a direct reflection upon an improvement in the quality of our government. Life has essential quality. But we begin to lose quality as the governments make us sacrifice quality for forms of security. In the enlightened age that I envision coming, there will be more emphasis on personal freedom; hence, more quality in our own lives.

Starting in the late '60s, and certainly by the tail-end of the '70s, it became popular to be negative about America, to kick sand in her face. It became unfashionable to think that America was still the greatest country on the face of the Earth. Unfortunately, that seemed to be a myth that fed upon itself.

In fact, if you've done any traveling at all throughout the world, you know that America is still the greatest place there is. There is simply nothing finer than this country. Things work here. People work here. The life-style here is, literally, light years ahead of the life-style of any other country on the globe.

Nonetheless, there appears to be a group of people who find contentment in belittling and tearing down America and her economy, instead of working positively on building her up. To those people, I only wish they would commit to memory the following poem:

I saw them tearing a building down,
A gang of men in my home town.
With a heave and a ho and a yes, yes, yell,
They swung a beam, and a side wall fell.

I said to the foreman, "Are these men skilled,
As the ones you'd use if you had to build?"
He laughed and said, "Ah, no indeed,
Common labor is all I need.

"Boy, I can destroy in a day or two
What it takes a builder ten years to do."
I said to myself, as I went my way,
"Which of these roles am I willing to play?"

It is so terribly easy to tear down an idea, concept, or individual. It takes no skill, no ability; just a few negative comments. But that negativism accomplishes nothing. It doesn't get anything done. It doesn't contribute to the well-being of our fellow man. What does contribute to our lives and to our country is an outrageously positive view towards the future, towards ourselves, and towards our economic activities.

I wish that in our pledge of allegiance to the American flag, we would also have a pledge of allegiance to be positive; a pledge of allegiance to take on challenges of the future and problems of the past, and create opportunities for the betterment of our world. Deep within my bones I feel that America has reached a turning point. As a nation, I feel we will again assume the responsibilities handed to us, and respond in an upbeat way.

The next twenty years are going to be happy ones, and especially happy ones for the wise investor who takes the time to do a little positive investment scheming, some reflection, and plan ahead for coming changes. I wish you good luck and encourage you to make things happen.